America's Favorite Brand Name
BAKING

Publications International, Ltd.

America's Favorite Brand Name
BAKING

Memorable Cakes

You'll find fabulous recipes for moist chocolate cake, spicy carrot cake, classic sour cream pound cake and more in this collection of delightful cakes.

White Chocolate Cheesecake

½ cup (1 stick) butter or margarine
¾ cup sugar, divided
1½ teaspoon vanilla, divided
1 cup flour
4 packages (8 ounces each) PHILADELPHIA BRAND® Cream Cheese, softened
4 eggs
2 packages (6 ounces each) BAKER'S® Premium White Chocolate Baking Squares, melted, slightly cooled

MIX butter, ¼ cup of the sugar and ½ teaspoon of the vanilla with electric mixer on medium speed until light and fluffy. Gradually add flour, mixing on low speed until blended. Press onto bottom of 9-inch springform pan; prick with fork. Bake at 325°F for 25 minutes or until edges are light golden brown.

MIX cream cheese, remaining ½ cup sugar and 1 teaspoon vanilla with electric mixer on medium speed until well blended. Add eggs, 1 at a time, mixing on low speed after each addition just until blended. Blend in melted chocolate. Pour over crust.

BAKE at 325°F for 55 minutes to 1 hour or until center is almost set. Run knife or metal spatula around rim of pan to loosen cake; cool before removing rim of pan. Refrigerate 4 hours or overnight. Garnish, if desired.   *Makes 12 servings*

Prep time: 35 minutes plus refrigerating
Bake time: 1 hour

White Chocolate Macadamia Nut Cheesecake: Stir 1 jar (3½ ounces) macadamia nuts, chopped (about ¾ cup), into batter.

White Chocolate Cheesecake

Mom's Favorite White Cake

Mom's Favorite White Cake

2¼ cups cake flour
1 tablespoon baking powder
½ teaspoon salt
1½ cups sugar
½ cup butter or margarine, softened
4 egg whites
2 teaspoons vanilla
1 cup milk
   Strawberry Frosting (recipe follows)
   Fruit Filling (recipe follows)
   Fresh strawberries (optional)

PREHEAT oven to 350°F. Line bottoms of two 9-inch round cake pans with waxed paper; lightly grease paper. Combine flour, baking powder and salt in medium bowl.

BEAT sugar and butter in large bowl with electric mixer at medium speed until light and fluffy. Add egg whites, two at a time, beating well after each addition. Add vanilla; beat until blended. At low speed, add flour mixture alternately with milk, beating well after each addition. Pour batter evenly into prepared pans.

BAKE 25 minutes or until wooden pick inserted into centers comes out clean. Cool layers in pans on wire rack 10 minutes. Loosen edges and invert layers onto racks to cool completely.

PREPARE Strawberry Frosting and Fruit Filling. To fill and frost cake, place one layer on cake plate; spread top with Fruit Filling. Place second layer over filling. Frost top and sides with Strawberry Frosting. Place strawberries on top of cake, if desired. Refrigerate; allow cake to stand at room temperature 15 minutes before serving.   *Makes 12 servings*

Strawberry Frosting

2 envelopes (1.3 ounces each)
   whipped topping mix
⅔ cup milk
1 cup (6 ounces) white chocolate
   chips, melted
¼ cup strawberry jam

BEAT whipped topping mix and milk in medium bowl with electric mixer on low speed until blended. Beat on high speed 4 minutes until topping thickens and forms peaks. With mixer at low speed, beat melted chocolate into topping. Add jam; beat until blended. Chill 15 minutes or until spreading consistency.

Fruit Filling

1 cup Strawberry Frosting (recipe
   above)
1 can (8 ounces) crushed pineapple,
   drained
1 cup sliced strawberries

COMBINE Strawberry Frosting, pineapple and strawberries in medium bowl; mix well.

Spicy Gingerbread

2 cups all-purpose flour
1 cup light molasses
¾ cup buttermilk
½ cup granulated sugar
½ cup FLEISCHMANN'S® 70% Corn
   Oil Spread, softened
¼ cup EGG BEATERS® Healthy Egg
   Substitute
2 teaspoons baking soda
1 teaspoon ground cinnamon
½ teaspoon ground ginger
¼ teaspoon ground cloves
   Powdered sugar, optional

In large bowl, with electric mixer at low speed, beat flour, molasses, buttermilk, granulated sugar, spread, Egg Beaters, baking soda, cinnamon, ginger and cloves until moistened; scrape side and bottom of bowl. Beat at medium speed for 3 minutes. Spread batter into greased 9-inch square baking pan. Bake at 350°F for 1 hour or until toothpick inserted in center comes out clean. Cool in pan on wire rack. Dust with powdered sugar before serving, if desired. Cut into 16 (2-inch) squares.

Makes 16 servings

Prep time: 20 minutes
Cook time: 1 hour

Philly 3-Step™ Fruit Topped Cheesecake

2 packages (8 ounces each)
   PHILADELPHIA BRAND® Cream
   Cheese, softened
½ cup sugar
½ teaspoon vanilla
2 eggs
1 ready-to-use graham cracker pie
   crust (6 ounces or 9 inches)
2 cups fresh fruit slices
2 tablespoons KRAFT® Strawberry
   or Apple Jelly, heated (optional)

1. MIX cream cheese, sugar and vanilla with electric mixer on medium speed until well blended. Add eggs; mix until blended.

2. POUR into crust.

3. BAKE at 350°F for 40 minutes or until center is almost set. Cool. Refrigerate 3 hours or overnight. Top with fruit; drizzle with jelly, if desired.   *Makes 8 servings*

Prep time: 10 minutes
Bake time: 40 minutes

Sour Cream Pound Cake

3 cups sugar
1 cup (2 sticks) butter, softened
1 teaspoon vanilla
1 teaspoon lemon extract
6 eggs
3 cups cake flour
¼ teaspoon baking soda
1 cup dairy sour cream

Heat oven to 325°F. Butter and flour 10-inch tube pan. In large bowl, beat sugar and butter until light and fluffy. Add vanilla and lemon extract; mix well. Add eggs, one at a time, beating well after each addition. In medium bowl, combine flour and baking soda. Add to butter mixture alternately with sour cream, beating well after each addition. Pour batter into pan. Bake 1 hour and 20 minutes or until toothpick inserted in center comes out clean. Cool in pan 15 minutes; invert onto wire rack and cool completely. Store tightly covered. *Makes 16 to 20 servings*

Favorite recipe from **Southeast United Dairy Industry Association, Inc.**

BAKING SECRET

If cake layers cool too long in baking pans, they will be difficult to remove. If this happens simply place the pans in a preheated 350°F oven for 3 to 5 minutes, then turn the layers out onto wire racks.

Fudge Truffle Cheesecake

Chocolate Crumb Crust (recipe follows)
2 cups (12-ounce package) HERSHEY'S® Semi-Sweet Chocolate Chips
3 packages (8 ounces each) cream cheese, softened
1 can (14 ounces) sweetened condensed milk (not evaporated milk)
4 eggs
2 teaspoons vanilla extract

Prepare Chocolate Crumb Crust. Heat oven to 300°F. In microwave-safe bowl, place chocolate chips. Microwave at HIGH (100%) 1½ minutes; stir. If necessary, microwave at HIGH an additional 15 seconds at a time, stirring after each heating, just until chips are melted when stirred. In large bowl, beat cream cheese until fluffy. Gradually beat in sweetened condensed milk until smooth. Add melted chips, eggs and vanilla; mix well. Pour into prepared crust. Bake 1 hour and 5 minutes or until center is set. Remove from oven to wire rack. With knife, loosen cake from side of pan. Cool completely; remove side of pan. Refrigerate several hours before serving. Garnish as desired. Cover; refrigerate leftover cheesecake.
Makes 10 to 12 servings

Chocolate Crumb Crust: In medium bowl, stir together 1½ cups vanilla wafer crumbs, ½ cup powdered sugar, ⅓ cup HERSHEY'S® Cocoa and ⅓ cup melted butter or margarine. Press firmly onto bottom of 9-inch springform pan.

Sour Cream Pound Cake

Karen Ann's Lemon Cake

2 cups all-purpose flour
1½ teaspoons baking powder
½ teaspoon baking soda
¼ teaspoon salt
⅔ cup butter or margarine, softened
1¼ cups granulated sugar
3 eggs, separated
¾ cup sour cream
Grated peel of 1 SUNKIST® Lemon
Lemony Frosting (recipe follows)

Line two 8-inch round cake pans with waxed paper. Preheat oven to 350°F. In medium bowl, combine flour, baking powder, baking soda and salt. In large bowl, with electric mixer, cream butter and sugar. Beat in egg yolks one at a time; beat until light in color. Add flour mixture alternately with sour cream, beating just until smooth. With clean beaters, beat egg whites until soft peaks form. Fold beaten egg whites and lemon peel into batter. Pour batter into prepared pans. Bake at 350°F for 30 to 35 minutes or until wooden pick inserted in center comes out clean. Cool 10 minutes. Remove from pans and peel off waxed paper. Cool on wire racks. Fill and frost with Lemony Frosting.

Makes 12 servings

Lemony Frosting

½ cup butter or margarine, softened
3 cups confectioners' sugar, divided
Grated peel of ½ SUNKIST® Lemon
2 tablespoons fresh squeezed lemon juice

In medium bowl, cream together butter and 1 cup confectioners' sugar. Add lemon peel, lemon juice and remaining 2 cups sugar; beat until smooth.

Makes about 1¾ cups frosting

Frosted Peanut Butter Cake Squares

About 30 REESE'S® Peanut Butter Cup Miniatures
⅓ cup butter or margarine, softened
½ cup REESE'S® Creamy or Crunchy Peanut Butter
⅓ cup granulated sugar
⅓ cup packed light brown sugar
½ cup milk
2 eggs
1 teaspoon vanilla extract
1 cup all-purpose flour
1 teaspoon baking soda
¼ teaspoon salt
Chocolate Peanut Butter Topping (recipe follows)

Heat oven to 350°F. Remove wrappers from candies. Chop candies into pieces. Grease 13×9×2-inch baking pan. In small mixer bowl, beat butter, peanut butter, granulated sugar and brown sugar until well blended. Gradually add milk, eggs and vanilla, beating until smooth and well blended. Stir together flour, baking soda and salt. Add to butter mixture; beat until well blended. Spread batter into prepared pan. Bake 18 to 20 minutes or until wooden pick inserted in center comes out clean. Cool completely in pan on wire rack. Prepare Chocolate Peanut Butter Topping; spread over cake. Sprinkle candy pieces over top. Cut into squares.

Makes 12 to 14 servings

Chocolate Peanut Butter Topping

½ cup HERSHEY'S® Semi-Sweet Chocolate Chips
⅓ cup REESE'S® Creamy Peanut Butter
2 tablespoons butter or margarine
¼ cup powdered sugar

In medium microwave-safe bowl, place chocolate chips, peanut butter and butter. Microwave at HIGH (100%) 1 minute; stir. If necessary, microwave at HIGH an additional 15 seconds at a time, stirring after each addition, just until chips are melted when stirred. Add powdered sugar; whisk until smooth and of spreading consistency.

BAKING SECRET

For easier frosting and decorating, place cooled cake layers in the freezer for 30 to 45 minutes before frosting.

Chocolate Mayonnaise Cake

2 cups all-purpose flour
⅔ cup unsweetened cocoa
1¼ teaspoons baking soda
¼ teaspoon baking powder
3 eggs
1⅔ cups sugar
1 teaspoon vanilla
1 cup HELLMANN'S® or BEST FOODS® Real or Light Mayonnaise or Low Fat Mayonnaise Dressing
1⅓ cups water

Grease and flour bottoms of two 9×1½-inch round cake pans. In medium bowl, combine flour, cocoa, baking soda and baking powder; set aside. In large bowl with mixer at high speed, beat eggs, sugar and vanilla, scraping bowl occasionally, 3 minutes or until smooth and creamy. Reduce speed to low; beat in mayonnaise until blended. Add flour mixture in 4 additions alternately with water, beginning and ending with flour mixture. Pour into prepared pans. Bake in 350°F oven 30 to 35 minutes or until cake springs back when touched lightly in center. Cool in pans on wire racks 10 minutes. Remove from pans; cool completely on racks. Fill and frost as desired.

Makes 1 (9-inch) layer cake

Spicy Butterscotch Snack Cake

1 cup (2 sticks) butter or margarine, softened
1 cup sugar
2 eggs
½ teaspoon vanilla extract
½ cup applesauce
2½ cups all-purpose flour
1½ to 2 teaspoons ground cinnamon
1 teaspoon baking soda
½ teaspoon salt
1⅔ cups (10-ounce package) HERSHEY'S® Butterscotch Chips
1 cup chopped pecans (optional)
Powdered sugar (optional)

Heat oven to 350°F. Lightly grease 13×9×2-inch baking pan. In large mixer bowl, beat butter and sugar until light and fluffy. Add eggs and vanilla; beat well. Mix in applesauce. Stir together flour, cinnamon, baking soda and salt; gradually add to butter mixture, mixing well. Stir in butterscotch chips and pecans, if desired. Spread into prepared pan. Bake 35 to 40 minutes or until wooden pick inserted in center comes out clean. Cool completely in pan on wire rack. Sprinkle with powdered sugar, if desired.

Makes 12 servings

German Sweet Chocolate Cake

1 package (4 ounces) BAKER'S®
    GERMAN'S Sweet Chocolate
½ cup water
2 cups all-purpose flour
1 teaspoon baking soda
¼ teaspoon salt
1 cup (2 sticks) butter or margarine,
    softened
2 cups sugar
4 egg yolks
1 teaspoon vanilla
1 cup buttermilk
4 egg whites
    Classic Coconut-Pecan Filling and
    Frosting (recipe follows)

HEAT oven to 350°F. Line bottoms of 3 (9-inch) round cake pans with waxed paper.

MICROWAVE chocolate and water in large microwavable bowl on HIGH 1½ to 2 minutes or until chocolate is almost melted, stirring halfway through heating time. *Stir until chocolate is completely melted.*

MIX flour, baking soda and salt; set aside. Beat butter and sugar in large bowl with electric mixer on medium speed until light and fluffy. Add egg yolks, 1 at a time, beating well after each addition. Stir in chocolate mixture and vanilla. Add flour mixture alternately with buttermilk, beating after each addition until smooth.

BEAT egg whites in another large bowl with electric mixer on high speed until they form stiff peaks. Gently stir into batter. Pour batter into prepared pans.

BAKE 30 minutes or until cake springs back when lightly touched in center. Immediately run spatula between cakes and sides of pans. Cool in pans 15 minutes. Remove from pans. Peel off waxed paper. Cool completely on wire racks.

SPREAD Classic Coconut-Pecan Filling and Frosting between layers and over top of cake. *Makes 12 servings*

Prep time: 40 minutes
Cook time: 30 minutes

Classic Coconut-Pecan Filling and Frosting

1 can (12 ounces) evaporated milk
1½ cups sugar
¾ cup (1½ sticks) butter or
    margarine
4 egg yolks, slightly beaten
1½ teaspoons vanilla
1 package (7 ounces) BAKER'S®
    ANGEL FLAKE® Coconut (about
    2⅔ cups)
1½ cups chopped pecans

STIR milk, sugar, butter, egg yolks and vanilla in large saucepan. Cook over medium heat until mixture thickens and is golden brown, about 12 minutes, stirring constantly. Remove from heat.

STIR in coconut and pecans. Cool until room temperature and of spreading consistency. *Makes about 4¼ cups*

Prep time: 20 minutes

From top: German Sweet Chocolate Cake, Wellesley Fudge Cake (page 16)

Wellesley Fudge Cake

4 squares BAKER'S® Unsweetened
    Chocolate
1¾ cups sugar, divided
½ cup water
1⅔ cups all-purpose flour
1 teaspoon baking soda
¼ teaspoon salt
½ cup (1 stick) butter or margarine,
    softened
3 eggs
¾ cup milk
1 teaspoon vanilla

HEAT oven to 350°F.

MICROWAVE chocolate, ½ cup sugar and water in large microwavable bowl on HIGH 1 to 2 minutes or until chocolate is almost melted, stirring halfway through heating time. Stir until chocolate is completely melted; cool.

MIX flour, baking soda and salt; set aside. Beat butter and remaining 1¼ cups sugar in large bowl with electric mixer on medium speed until light and fluffy. Add eggs, 1 at a time, beating well after each addition. Add flour mixture alternately with milk, beating after each addition until smooth. Stir in chocolate mixture and vanilla. Pour into 2 greased and floured 9-inch round cake pans.

BAKE 30 to 35 minutes or until cake springs back when lightly touched. Cool 10 minutes; remove from pans. Cool on wire racks. Frost as desired.

Makes 12 servings

Prep time: 30 minutes
Cook time: 35 minutes

Carrot Layer Cake

CAKE
1 package DUNCAN HINES® Moist
    Deluxe Yellow Cake Mix
4 eggs
½ cup CRISCO® Oil or CRISCO®
    PURITAN® Canola Oil
3 cups grated carrots
1 cup finely chopped nuts
2 teaspoons ground cinnamon

CREAM CHEESE FROSTING
1 (8-ounce) package cream cheese,
    softened
¼ cup butter or margarine, softened
2 teaspoons vanilla extract
4 cups confectioners sugar

1. Preheat oven to 350°F. Grease and flour 2 (8- or 9-inch) round baking pans.

2. For cake, combine cake mix, eggs, oil, carrots, nuts and cinnamon in large bowl. Beat at low speed with electric mixer until moistened. Beat at medium speed for 2 minutes. Pour into pans. Bake at 350°F for 35 to 40 minutes or until toothpick inserted in centers comes out clean. Cool.

3. For frosting, place cream cheese, butter and vanilla extract in large bowl. Beat at low speed until smooth and creamy. Add confectioners sugar gradually, beating until smooth. Add more sugar to thicken, or milk or water to thin frosting, as needed. Fill and frost cooled cake. Garnish with whole pecans.

Makes 12 to 16 servings

Carrot Layer Cake

Lemon Cream Almond Torte

TORTE
- ½ cup sifted cake flour
- ½ teaspoon baking powder
- ⅛ teaspoon salt
- ½ cup softened butter
- ¾ cup granulated sugar
- 1 cup BLUE DIAMOND® Blanched Almond Paste
- 3 eggs
- 1 tablespoon brandy
- 1 teaspoon vanilla extract
- ⅛ teaspoon almond extract

LEMON CREAM
- 3 egg yolks
- ⅓ cup granulated sugar
- 2 tablespoons flour
- 1 cup milk, scalded
- 2 teaspoons grated lemon peel
- 2 tablespoons lemon juice
- ½ teaspoon vanilla extract

GARNISH
Powdered sugar

Sift together flour, baking powder and salt; set aside. Cream butter and sugar. Add almond paste and beat until mixture is smooth. Add eggs one at a time, beating well after each addition. Mix in brandy, vanilla and almond extract. On lowest speed, add flour mixture. Pour into a greased and floured 8-inch round cake pan (at least 2 inches deep) or springform pan. Bake at 325°F. for 45 minutes or until a toothpick inserted in center comes out clean. Cool in pan 15 minutes. Remove and cool right-side up on wire rack.

Meanwhile, prepare Lemon Cream. Beat yolks and sugar until mixture is thick and pale yellow. Stir in flour. Gradually pour hot milk into egg mixture, whisking constantly. Stir in grated lemon peel. Boil mixture 1 minute, whisking constantly. Remove from heat, add lemon juice and vanilla; stir until cooled. Slice cake into 2 layers. Spread Lemon Cream over bottom layer; top with second layer. Place a lace doily over top of torte. Sift powdered sugar evenly over top and carefully remove doily. Chill. *Makes 8 to 10 servings*

Philly 3-Step™ Caramel Pecan Cheesecake

- 2 packages (8 ounces each) PHILADELPHIA BRAND® Cream Cheese, softened
- ½ cup sugar
- ½ teaspoon vanilla
- 2 eggs
- 20 caramels
- 2 tablespoons milk
- ½ cup chopped pecans
- 1 ready-to-use graham cracker pie crust (6 ounces or 9 inches)

1. **MIX** cream cheese, sugar and vanilla with electric mixer on medium speed until well blended. Add eggs; mix until blended. Melt caramels with milk in small saucepan on low heat, stirring frequently until smooth. Stir in pecans.

2. **POUR** caramel mixture into crust. Pour cream cheese batter over caramel mixture.

3. **BAKE** at 350°F for 40 minutes or until center is almost set. Cool. Refrigerate 3 hours or overnight. Garnish, if desired. *Makes 8 servings*

Prep time: 10 minutes
Bake time: 40 minutes

Chocolate Caramel Pecan Cheesecake: Blend 4 squares BAKER'S® Semi-Sweet Chocolate, melted and slightly cooled, into batter. Continue as directed.

Brownie Sundae Cake

1 19- to 21-ounce package fudge brownie mix, prepared according to package directions for cake-like brownies
1 cup "M & M's"® Semi-Sweet Chocolate Mini Baking Bits
½ cup chopped nuts, optional
1 quart vanilla ice cream, softened
¼ cup caramel or butterscotch ice cream topping

Line 2 (9-inch) round cake pans with aluminum foil, extending slightly over edges of pans. Lightly spray bottoms with vegetable cooking spray; set aside. Preheat oven as brownie mix package directs. Divide brownie batter evenly between pans; sprinkle ½ cup "M & M's"® Semi-Sweet Chocolate Mini Baking Bits and ¼ cup nuts, if using, over each pan. Bake 23 to 25 minutes or until edges begin to pull away from sides of pan. Cool completely. Remove layers by lifting foil from pans.

To assemble cake, place one brownie layer, topping side down in 9-inch springform pan. Carefully spread ice cream over brownie layer; drizzle with ice cream topping. Place second brownie layer on top of ice cream layer, topping side up; press down lightly. Cover with plastic wrap and freeze until firm. Remove from freezer about 15 minutes before serving. Remove side of pan. Cut into wedges. *Makes 12 servings*

Brownie Sundae Cake

Irresistible Pies & Tarts

Freshly baked apple pie cooling in the kitchen, rich and gooey pecan pie and spicy pumpkin pie all remind us of happy occasions shared with family and friends. Continue to celebrate the good times with these irresistible pies and tarts.

Fruit Tart

⅓ cup FLEISCHMANN'S® 70% Corn Oil Spread
1¼ cups all-purpose flour
4 to 5 tablespoons ice water
1 cup EGG BEATERS® Healthy Egg Substitute
⅓ cup sugar
1 teaspoon vanilla extract
1¼ cups skim milk, scalded
1 cup sliced fresh fruit

In medium bowl, cut spread into flour until mixture resembles coarse crumbs. Add water, 1 tablespoon at a time, tossing until moistened. Shape into a ball. On floured surface, roll dough into 11-inch circle, about ⅛ inch thick. Place in 9-inch pie plate, making a ½-inch-high fluted edge; set aside.

In medium bowl, combine Egg Beaters, sugar and vanilla; gradually stir in milk. Pour into prepared crust. Bake at 350°F for 45 to 50 minutes or until set. Cool completely on wire rack. Cover; chill until firm, about 2 hours. To serve, top with fruit.

Makes 10 servings

Prep time: 30 minutes
Cook time: 45 minutes

Rolling out a pastry crust is a breeze with a canvas pastry cloth. Simply dust the cloth generously with flour and roll out the dough to the appropriate size. Always wash the cloth after each use.

Fruit Tart

Classic Pecan Pie

3 eggs
1 cup sugar
1 cup KARO® Light or Dark Corn
    Syrup
2 tablespoons MAZOLA® margarine
    or butter, melted
1 teaspoon vanilla
1½ cups pecans
    Easy-As-Pie Crust (page 29) or
        1 (9-inch) frozen deep dish pie
        crust*

*To use prepared frozen pie crust: Do not thaw. Preheat oven and a cookie sheet. Pour filling into frozen crust. Bake on cookie sheet.

Preheat oven to 350°F. In medium bowl with fork beat eggs slightly. Add sugar, corn syrup, margarine and vanilla; stir until well blended. Stir in pecans. Pour into pie crust.

Bake 50 to 55 minutes or until knife inserted halfway between center and edge comes out clean. Cool on wire rack.

Makes 8 servings

Prep time: 6 minutes
Bake time: 50 minutes, plus cooling

Almond Amaretto Pie: Substitute 1 cup sliced almonds for pecans. Add 2 tablespoons almond flavored liqueur and ½ teaspoon almond extract to filling.

Butterscotch Pecan Pie: Omit margarine; add ¼ cup heavy or whipping cream to filling.

Chocolate Chip Walnut Pie: Substitute 1 cup walnuts, coarsely chopped, for pecans. Sprinkle ½ cup semisweet chocolate chips over bottom of pie crust. Carefully pour filling into pie crust.

BAKING SECRET

To measure flour accurately, spoon it into a dry measure until the measure is overflowing. Then with a straight-edged metal spatula, sweep across the top of the measure. Do not scoop the flour with the measure or tap the measure on the counter, because this will compact the flour and result in an inaccurate measure.

Country Fruit Pie

2 pie crust sticks
5 fresh California peaches or
    nectarines, each cut into
    8 slices (about 3 cups)
3 fresh California plums, each cut
    into 6 slices (about 1 cup)
⅓ cup honey
3 tablespoons all-purpose flour
½ teaspoon almond extract

Preheat oven to 400°F. Roll out 1 pie crust stick according to package directions to fit 8-inch pie dish. Roll out remaining pie crust stick; cut out about 35 leaf shapes with small leaf-shaped cutter. Gently toss fruit, honey, flour and almond extract in large bowl. Spoon fruit mixture into crust. Place 8 leaf cut-outs over fruit; press remaining leaves onto rim of pie crust with small amount of water. Bake 25 to 30 minutes or until crust is browned and fruit is easily pierced with knife.

Makes 8 servings

Favorite recipe from **California Tree Fruit Agreement**

**From top: Almond Amaretto Pie,
Classic Pecan Pie**

Hazelnut Plum Tart

1 cup hazelnuts
¼ cup firmly packed light brown
    sugar
1 cup all-purpose flour
⅓ cup FILIPPO BERIO® Olive Oil
1 egg, separated
    Pinch salt
3 tablespoons granulated sugar
2 teaspoons cornstarch
½ teaspoon grated lime peel
    Pinch ground nutmeg
    Pinch ground cloves
1¼ pounds plums (about 5 large),
    halved and pitted
3 tablespoons currant jelly
    Sweetened whipped cream
    (optional)

Preheat oven to 375°F. Grease 9-inch tart
pan with removable bottom with olive oil.

Place hazelnuts in food processor;
process until coarsely chopped. Remove
¼ cup for garnish; set aside. Add brown

sugar; process until nuts are finely ground.
Add flour, olive oil, egg yolk and salt;
process until combined. (Mixture will be
crumbly.)

Spoon mixture into prepared pan. Press
firmly in even layer on bottom and up side.
Brush inside of crust with slightly beaten
egg white. Place crust in freezer
10 minutes.

In large bowl, combine granulated sugar,
cornstarch, lime peel, nutmeg and cloves.
Cut each plum half into 4 wedges. Add to
sugar mixture; toss until combined.
Arrange plums in overlapping circles in
crust; spoon any remaining sugar mixture
over plums. Place tart on baking sheet.

Bake 45 to 50 minutes or until fruit is
tender and juices are thickened. Cool
30 minutes on wire rack. Place currant
jelly in small saucepan; heat over low heat,
stirring frequently, until melted. Brush over
plums; sprinkle with reserved hazelnuts.
Serve tart warm or at room temperature
with whipped cream, if desired.

Makes 6 servings

Hazelnut Plum Tart

Chocolate Brandy Pie

PIE SHELL
1¼ cups all-purpose flour
1 tablespoon sugar
½ teaspoon salt
6 tablespoons butter
1 egg
1 to 2 tablespoons water

FILLING
¼ cup all-purpose flour
½ teaspoon baking soda
Pinch salt
¾ cup strong coffee
¼ cup brandy
½ cup butter
2 ounces unsweetened chocolate
1 cup BLUE DIAMOND® Blanched Almond Paste
1 cup sugar
1 egg, beaten
½ teaspoon vanilla extract
½ teaspoon almond extract

GARNISH
Whipped cream
Chocolate shavings

To prepare pie shell in food processor, combine flour, sugar and salt. Add butter and mix with on-off bursts until mixture resembles coarse cornmeal.* *Do not overmix.* Add egg and enough water just to form dough. Shape dough into ball and chill 30 minutes. Roll dough out on lightly floured board. Fit into 9-inch pie pan; chill 30 minutes. Prick bottom of pastry shell with fork. Line with waxed paper and fill with dried beans. Bake at 400°F. for 10 minutes. Remove paper and beans; reserve shell.

To prepare filling, sift flour, baking soda and salt; set aside. In a double boiler, over simmering water, heat coffee and brandy. Add butter and chocolate, stirring until melted and smooth. Remove from heat;

set aside. Beat almond paste and sugar until mixture resembles coarse cornmeal. Add egg and extracts, beating until smooth. Blend in flour mixture. Gradually add chocolate mixture, scraping sides of bowl occasionally. Pour into prepared pie shell. Bake at 275°F. for 1½ hours. Cool on wire rack. Garnish with whipped cream and chocolate shavings.

Makes 8 to 10 servings

*To prepare by hand, combine flour, sugar and salt. With fingertips or pastry cutter, work butter into flour mixture until mixture resembles coarse cornmeal.

Praline Pie

1 (9-inch) HONEY MAID® Honey Graham Pie Crust
1 egg white, slightly beaten
¼ cup margarine, melted
1 cup firmly packed light brown sugar
¾ cup all-purpose flour
1 teaspoon baking powder
1 egg
1 teaspoon vanilla extract
1 cup PLANTERS® Pecans, coarsely chopped
Prepared whipped topping, for garnish

Preheat oven to 375°F. Brush pie crust with egg white. Bake at 375°F for 5 minutes; set aside. *Decrease oven temperature to 350°F.*

In medium bowl, with electric mixer at low speed, beat margarine and brown sugar until blended. Mix in flour, baking powder, egg and vanilla until well combined. Stir in ¾ cup pecans. Spread in prepared crust; sprinkle top with remaining ¼ cup pecans. Bake at 350°F for 25 to 30 minutes or until lightly browned and filling is set. Cool completely on wire rack. Garnish with whipped topping. *Makes 6 servings*

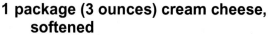

Pumpkin Cheese-Swirled Pie

1 package (3 ounces) cream cheese, softened
½ cup KARO® Light Corn Syrup, divided
½ teaspoon vanilla
1 cup canned solid pack pumpkin
2 eggs
½ cup evaporated milk
¼ cup sugar
2 teaspoons pumpkin pie spice
¼ teaspoon salt
Easy-As-Pie Crust (page 29) or 1 (9-inch) frozen deep dish pie crust*

*To use prepared frozen pie crust: Do not thaw. Preheat oven and a cookie sheet. Pour filling into frozen crust. Bake on cookie sheet.

Preheat oven to 325°F. In small bowl with mixer at medium speed, beat cream cheese until light and fluffy. Gradually beat in ¼ cup corn syrup and vanilla until smooth; set aside. In medium bowl combine pumpkin, eggs, evaporated milk, remaining ¼ cup corn syrup, sugar, pumpkin pie spice and salt. Beat until smooth. Pour into pie crust. Drop tablespoonfuls of cream cheese mixture onto pumpkin filling. With knife or small spatula, swirl mixture to give marbled effect.

Bake 50 to 60 minutes or until knife inserted halfway between edge and center comes out clean. Cool completely on wire rack. *Makes 8 servings*

Prep time: 20 minutes
Bake time: 50 minutes, plus cooling

Peanut Butter Crumble Topped Apple Pie

1 cup (8 ounces) dairy sour cream
¾ cup sugar, divided
2 eggs
2 tablespoons plus ¾ cup all-purpose flour, divided
2 teaspoons vanilla extract
¼ teaspoon salt
4 cups peeled, thinly sliced apples (about 5 apples)
1 unbaked 9-inch pie crust
1 cup quick-cooking or regular rolled oats
1 teaspoon ground cinnamon
1 cup REESE'S® Creamy Peanut Butter
1 tablespoon butter or margarine, softened

Heat oven to 350°F. In large bowl, with whisk, blend sour cream, ½ cup sugar, eggs, 2 tablespoons flour, vanilla and salt. Add apples; stir until well coated. Spoon into unbaked crust. Stir together oats, remaining ¾ cup flour, remaining ¼ cup sugar and cinnamon. In small microwave-safe bowl, place peanut butter and butter. Microwave at HIGH (100%) 30 seconds or until butter is melted. Stir mixture until smooth. Add to oat mixture; blend until crumbs are formed. Sprinkle crumb mixture over apples. Bake 55 to 60 minutes or until apples are tender and topping is golden brown. Cool completely on wire rack. Cover; refrigerate leftover pie. *Makes 6 to 8 servings*

Nectarine Pecan Tart

PECAN CRUST
- 1 cup vanilla wafer crumbs
- ½ cup pecan pieces
- 2 tablespoons sugar
- 3 tablespoons unsalted butter, melted

CREAM CHEESE FILLING
- 1 (8-ounce) package plus 1 (3-ounce) package cream cheese, softened
- 3 tablespoons sugar
- 2 tablespoons orange juice
- ½ teaspoon vanilla

FRUIT TOPPING
- 2 ripe nectarines
- 4 tablespoons apricot jelly

1. For crust, preheat oven to 350°F. Process wafer crumbs, pecans and sugar in food processor until coarse crumbs form. Transfer to small bowl; stir in butter. Pat evenly on bottom and 1 inch up side of 8-inch springform pan. Bake 15 minutes or until lightly browned. Cool completely on wire rack.

2. For filling, beat cream cheese, sugar, juice and vanilla in medium bowl with electric mixer at low speed until blended. Increase speed to high; beat 2 minutes or until fluffy. Pour into crust. Cover; refrigerate 3 hours or until set.

3. For topping, halve and thinly slice nectarines. Arrange over filling.

4. To complete recipe, remove side of pan from tart; place tart on serving platter. Melt jelly in small saucepan, stirring constantly, over low heat. Cool 1 minute. Drizzle jelly over nectarines. Refrigerate, uncovered, until set. *Makes 6 servings*

Amaretto Cheesecake Tart

CRUST
- ¾ cup amaretti cookie crumbs
- ¾ cup zwieback crumbs
- 1 tablespoon sugar
- ¼ cup Prune Purée (page 74) or prepared prune butter

FILLING
- 1 carton (16 ounces) nonfat cottage cheese
- 4 ounces fat-free cream cheese, softened
- 2 eggs
- 2 tablespoons almond-flavored liqueur

TOPPING & GLAZE
- 2 oranges, peeled and sliced into rounds
- 1 kiwifruit, peeled and sliced into rounds
- 2 tablespoons apple jelly, melted
  Fresh raspberries, orange peel and mint leaves, for garnish

Preheat oven to 325°F. To prepare crust, in medium bowl, combine crumbs and sugar. Cut in prune purée with pastry blender until mixture resembles coarse crumbs. Press onto bottom and up side of 9-inch tart pan with removable bottom. To prepare filling, process cottage cheese and cream cheese in food processor 3 to 5 minutes or until smooth. Add eggs and liqueur; process until blended. Pour into prepared crust. Bake in center of oven 30 minutes until filling is set. Cool on wire rack; refrigerate until completely chilled. Arrange fruit on top of filling. Brush fruit with jelly. Garnish with raspberries, orange peel and mint. Cut into wedges. *Makes 10 servings*

Favorite recipe from **California Prune Board**

Noreen's Favorite Walnut Pie

3 eggs, lightly beaten
1 cup sugar
1 cup dark corn syrup
2 tablespoons all-purpose flour
2 tablespoons butter, melted
1 teaspoon vanilla
1 (9-inch) unbaked pastry pie shell
1½ cups large pieces DIAMOND®
   Walnuts

Heat oven to 400°F. Combine eggs, sugar, corn syrup, flour, butter and vanilla; blend well. Pour into unbaked pie shell; arrange walnuts on top. Bake in lower third of oven at 400°F. for 15 minutes. Reduce oven temperature to 350°F.; bake an additional 35 to 45 minutes or until center appears set. Cool completely.   *Makes 8 servings*

9-inch Classic Crisco® Double Crust

2 cups all-purpose flour
1 teaspoon salt
¾ CRISCO® Stick or ¾ cup CRISCO®
   all-vegetable shortening
5 tablespoons cold water

1. Spoon flour into measuring cup and level. Combine flour and salt in medium bowl.

2. Cut in shortening using pastry blender or 2 knives until flour is blended to form pea-size chunks.

3. Sprinkle with water, 1 tablespoon at a time. Toss lightly with fork until dough forms a ball.

4. Divide dough in half. Press half of dough between hands to form a 5- to 6-inch "pancake." Flour rolling surface and rolling pin lightly. Roll dough into circle.

Trim circle 1 inch larger than upside-down pie plate. Carefully remove trimmed dough. Set aside to reroll and use for pastry cutout garnish, if desired. Repeat with remaining half of dough.
Makes 2 (9-inch) crusts

Easy-As-Pie Crust

SINGLE PIE CRUST
1¼ cups unsifted flour
⅛ teaspoon salt
½ cup MAZOLA® Margarine
2 to 3 tablespoons cold water

In medium bowl combine flour and salt. With pastry blender or 2 knives, cut in margarine until mixture resembles fine crumbs. Sprinkle water over mixture while tossing to blend well. Press dough firmly into ball. On lightly floured surface, roll into 12-inch circle. Fit loosely into 9-inch pie plate. Trim and flute edge. Fill and bake according to recipe.
Makes one 9-inch crust

BAKING SECRET

To add a shiny golden glaze to the top crust of a fruit pie, brush with milk or an egg wash of 1 beaten egg and 1 tablespoon water just before baking. For a glossier darker color, substitute cream for the milk or an egg yolk for the whole egg. Delay brushing the decorative edge of the pie until the last 15 to 20 minutes of baking to avoid overbrowning.

Early American Pumpkin Pie

1½ cups cooked pumpkin, canned or fresh
1 cup whole or 2% milk
1 cup sugar
2 eggs, beaten
1 tablespoon butter or margarine, melted
½ teaspoon ground cinnamon
¼ teaspoon salt
¼ teaspoon ground ginger
¼ teaspoon ground nutmeg
1 (9-inch) unbaked pie shell
Sweetened whipped cream or whipped topping (optional)
Fresh currants (optional)

Preheat oven to 425°F. Combine pumpkin, milk, sugar, eggs, butter, cinnamon, salt, ginger and nutmeg in large bowl; blend well. Pour into pie shell. Bake 45 to 50 minutes or until knife inserted into filling comes out clean. Cool completely. Serve with whipped cream and garnish with currants, if desired. Refrigerate leftovers.
Makes 6 to 8 servings

Favorite recipe from **Bob Evans Farms®**

Golden Apple Pie with Rum Sauce

Pastry for 2-crust 9-inch pie
6 to 7 Golden Delicious apples
¼ cup firmly packed brown sugar
2 tablespoons all-purpose flour
½ teaspoon ground cinnamon
¼ teaspoon ground nutmeg
¼ teaspoon salt (optional)
¼ cup chopped nuts
Rum Sauce (recipe follows)

Line 9-inch pie plate with half of pastry; reserve remaining pastry. Peel, core and slice apples to equal 7 cups. In large bowl, combine apples, sugar, flour, cinnamon, nutmeg, salt and nuts. Transfer apple mixture to pastry-lined pie plate.

Preheat oven to 425°F. Roll out remaining pastry to 10-inch circle; cut into ¾-inch strips. Arrange strips in lattice pattern on top of apples and trim at edges; pinch edges of crusts together and flute.

Bake 20 minutes. *Reduce oven temperature to 375°F.* Bake 35 to 40 minutes or until apples are tender. If necessary, loosely cover top of pie with foil during baking to prevent overbrowning. Meanwhile, prepare Rum Sauce. To serve, cool pie at least 20 minutes; slice and serve with sauce. *Makes 10 servings*

Rum Sauce: In medium saucepan, combine 1 cup sugar, ¾ cup water and ½ teaspoon ground cinnamon. Bring to a boil over medium-high heat; boil 5 minutes, stirring occasionally. In small bowl, blend 2 tablespoons cornstarch and ¼ cup cold water; gradually stir into hot sugar mixture. Return to heat; cook, stirring constantly, until mixture bubbles and thickens. Remove from heat. Stir in ¼ cup rum. Serve warm.

Favorite recipe from **Washington Apple Commission**

BAKING SECRET

If a pie crust is browning too quickly, cover the edges with strips of foil. An alternative is to cut the bottom out of a foil pie pan and invert it over the pie.

Early American Pumpkin Pie

Country Apple Rhubarb Pie

CRUST
1 (9-inch) Classic CRISCO® Double Crust (page 29)

FILLING
9 cups sliced, peeled Granny Smith apples (about 3 pounds or 6 large apples)

1½ cups chopped (about ½-inch pieces) fresh rhubarb, peeled if tough

¾ cup granulated sugar

½ cup firmly packed light brown sugar

2 tablespoons all-purpose flour

1 tablespoon cornstarch

1 teaspoon ground cinnamon

¼ teaspoon freshly grated nutmeg

GLAZE
1 egg, beaten

1 tablespoon water

1 tablespoon granulated sugar

1 teaspoon ground pecans or walnuts

⅛ teaspoon ground cinnamon

1. For crust, prepare as directed. Roll and press bottom crust into 9- or 9½-inch deep-dish pie plate. *Do not bake.* Heat oven to 425°F.

2. For filling, combine apples and rhubarb in large bowl. Combine ¾ cup granulated sugar, brown sugar, flour, cornstarch, 1 teaspoon cinnamon and nutmeg in medium bowl. Sprinkle over fruit. Toss to coat. Spoon into unbaked pie crust. Moisten pastry edge with water. Cover pie with lattice top, cutting strips 1 inch wide. Flute edge high.

3. For glaze, combine egg and water in small bowl. Brush over crust. Combine remaining glaze ingredients in small bowl. Sprinkle over crust.

4. Bake at 425°F for 20 minutes. *Reduce oven temperature to 350°F.* Bake 30 to 40 minutes or until filling in center is bubbly and crust is golden brown. Place sheet of foil or baking sheet under pie if it starts to bubble over. Cool to room temperature.

Makes 1 (9- or 9½-inch) deep-dish pie

Traditional Cherry Pie

3 cups frozen tart cherries, not thawed

1 cup granulated sugar

2 tablespoons quick-cooking tapioca

½ teaspoon almond extract

Pastry for 2-crust (double) 9-inch pie

2 tablespoons butter or margarine

Preheat oven to 400°F. In medium bowl, combine cherries, sugar, tapioca and almond extract; mix well. Let cherry mixture stand 15 minutes.

Line 9-inch pie plate with 1 pastry crust; fill with cherry mixture. Dot with butter. Cover with top crust. Cut slits for steam to escape. Seal edges and flute.

Bake 50 to 55 minutes or until crust is golden brown and filling is bubbly.

Makes 6 to 8 servings

Favorite recipe from **Cherry Marketing Institute, Inc.**

Peach Delight Pie

FILLING
2½ **cups sliced, peeled peaches (about 1¼ pounds or 2 to 3 large)**
¾ **cup granulated sugar**
¼ **cup quick-cooking tapioca**
1 **teaspoon lemon juice**
1 **teaspoon peach-flavored brandy**

CRUMB MIXTURE
¼ **cup all-purpose flour**
¼ **cup packed brown sugar**
¼ **cup chopped almonds**
3 **tablespoons butter or margarine, melted**

CRUST
1 **9-inch Classic CRISCO® Double Crust (page 29)**

GLAZE
1 **egg white, slightly beaten**
Granulated sugar

1. For filling, combine peaches, ¾ cup granulated sugar, tapioca, lemon juice and brandy in medium bowl. Stir well. Let stand while making crumb mixture and crust.

2. For crumb mixture, combine flour, brown sugar, almonds and butter. Mix until crumbly. Heat oven to 425°F.

3. For crust, prepare as directed on page 29. Roll and press bottom crust into 9-inch pie plate. *Do not bake.* Sprinkle half of Crumb Mixture over unbaked pie crust. Add Filling. Top with remaining Crumb Mixture.

4. Cut out desired shapes from top crust with cookie cutter. Place on filling around edge of pie.

5. For glaze, brush cutouts with egg white. Sprinkle with granulated sugar. Cover edge of pie with foil to prevent overbrowning.

6. Bake at 425°F for 10 minutes. *Reduce oven temperature to 350°F.* Bake 25 minutes. Remove foil. Bake 5 minutes. Serve warm or at room temperature.

Makes 1 (9-inch) pie

BAKING SECRET

To prebake a pie or tart crust before filling it, prick the shell all over with a fork, line it with foil or parchment, and fill it with dried beans or rice. Bake the shell as directed removing the liner and beans during the last few minutes of baking to allow the crust to brown. The beans (or rice) can be cooled, stored in an airtight container and reused in the same way, but they should not be cooked and eaten. Ceramic or metal pie weights are also available.

Peach Delight Pie

Heavenly Brownies & Bars

Rich chocolaty brownies and sensational bar cookies have always been a special part of picnics and parties. With this collection of wonderful recipes, discover just how easy it is to serve those treats to your family.

Moist and Minty Brownies

1¼ **cups all-purpose flour**
½ **teaspoon baking soda**
¼ **teaspoon salt**
¾ **cup granulated sugar**
½ **cup (1 stick) butter or margarine**
2 **tablespoons water**
1½ **cups (10-ounce package) NESTLÉ® TOLL HOUSE® Mint-Chocolate Morsels, *divided***
1 **teaspoon vanilla extract**
2 **eggs**

COMBINE flour, baking soda and salt in small bowl. Combine sugar, butter and water in medium microwave-safe bowl. Microwave on HIGH (100%) power for 3 minutes, stirring halfway through cooking time. Stir until smooth. Add *1 cup* morsels and vanilla; stir until smooth. Add eggs, one at a time, stirring well after each addition. Stir in flour mixture and *remaining* morsels. Spread into greased 9-inch square baking pan.

BAKE in preheated 350°F. oven for 20 to 30 minutes or until center is set. Cool in pan on wire rack (center will sink).
Makes about 16 brownies

Saucepan method: COMBINE sugar, butter and water in medium saucepan. Bring *just to a boil* over medium heat, stirring constantly; remove from heat. Add *1 cup* morsels and vanilla; stir until smooth. Add eggs one at a time, stirring well after each addition. Stir in flour mixture and *remaining* morsels. Spread in pan; bake as directed above.

Moist and Minty Brownies

BAKING SECRET

For an easy glaze for bar cookies, sprinkle them with chocolate chips immediately after baking, then cover with foil. After 3 or 4 minutes, remove the foil and spread the melted chips over the bars.

Cherry Cheesecake Squares

2 cups graham cracker crumbs
1 cup sugar, divided
¼ cup (½ stick) butter or margarine, melted
3 packages (8 ounces each) PHILADELPHIA BRAND® Cream Cheese, softened
1 teaspoon vanilla
2 eggs
1 can (20 ounces) cherry pie filling

MIX crumbs, ¼ cup sugar and butter. Press into 13×9-inch baking pan. Bake at 325°F for 10 minutes.

MIX cream cheese, remaining ¾ cup sugar and vanilla with electric mixer on medium speed until well blended. Add eggs; mix just until blended. Pour over crust.

BAKE at 325°F for 35 minutes or until center is almost set. Cool. Refrigerate 3 hours or overnight. Top with pie filling. Cut into squares. Garnish, if desired.

Makes 18 squares

Prep time: 20 minutes plus refrigerating
Bake time: 35 minutes

Old-Fashioned Brownies

3 ounces (3 squares) unsweetened chocolate
½ cup shortening
1½ cups sugar
3 eggs
1½ teaspoons vanilla
¼ teaspoon salt
1 cup all-purpose flour
1½ cups chopped DIAMOND® Walnuts

VELVET CHOCOLATE ICING (OPTIONAL)
1 ounce (1 square) unsweetened chocolate, melted
2 tablespoons butter
2 tablespoons light corn syrup
1 cup powdered sugar
1 tablespoon milk
1 teaspoon vanilla

Heat oven to 325°F. Grease an 8-inch square baking pan. In top of double boiler over hot, not boiling, water, melt chocolate and shortening. Cool slightly. Combine sugar, eggs, vanilla and salt in large bowl; blend in chocolate mixture. Stir in flour; fold in walnuts. Spread in greased pan. Bake at 325°F. for about 40 minutes (brownies should still be soft). Cool completely in pan. If desired, prepare Velvet Chocolate Icing. Combine chocolate, butter and corn syrup; blend well. Add powdered sugar, milk and vanilla; blend well. Spread over brownies; cut into bars. *Makes 20 brownies*

Variation: Spread a thin layer of raspberry jam over top of hot brownies. Cool before spreading with icing.

Cherry Cheesecake Squares

Toffee Bars

1 cup butter or margarine, softened
1 cup firmly packed brown sugar
1 egg yolk
1 teaspoon vanilla
2 cups all-purpose flour
1 cup chopped DIAMOND® Walnuts, divided
½ cup semi-sweet chocolate pieces

Heat oven to 350°F. Grease 13×9-inch pan. Combine butter, brown sugar, egg yolk and vanilla; beat until light and fluffy. Stir in flour and ½ *cup* walnuts; spread in prepared pan. Bake at 350°F. for 25 minutes or until lightly browned. Immediately sprinkle with chocolate; spread over base when melted. Sprinkle chocolate with remaining ½ cup walnuts. Cool completely; cut into bars.

Makes 24 bars

P.B. Chips Brownie Cups

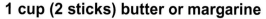

1 cup (2 sticks) butter or margarine
2 cups sugar
2 teaspoons vanilla extract
4 eggs
¾ cup HERSHEY'S® Cocoa or HERSHEY'S® European Style Cocoa
1¾ cups all-purpose flour
½ teaspoon baking powder
½ teaspoon salt
1⅔ cups (10-ounce package) REESE'S® Peanut Butter Chips, divided

1. Heat oven to 350°F. Line 18 muffin cups (2½ inches in diameter) with paper or foil bake cups.

2. In large microwave-safe bowl, place butter. Microwave at HIGH (100%) 1 to 1½ minutes or until melted. Stir in sugar and vanilla. Add eggs; beat well. Add cocoa; beat until well blended. Add flour, baking powder and salt; beat well. Stir in 1⅓ cups peanut butter chips. Divide batter evenly into muffin cups; sprinkle with remaining ⅓ cup peanut butter chips.

3. Bake 25 to 30 minutes or until surface is firm; cool completely in pan on wire rack.

Makes about 18 brownie cups

Bittersweet Brownies

MAZOLA® No Stick Cooking Spray
4 squares (1 ounce each) unsweetened chocolate, melted
1 cup sugar
½ cup HELLMANN'S® or BEST FOODS® Real or Light Mayonnaise or Low Fat Mayonnaise Dressing
2 eggs
1 teaspoon vanilla
¾ cup flour
½ teaspoon baking powder
¼ teaspoon salt
½ cup chopped walnuts

Preheat oven to 350°F. Spray 8×8×2-inch baking pan with cooking spray. In large bowl, stir chocolate, sugar, mayonnaise, eggs and vanilla until smooth. Stir in flour, baking powder and salt until well blended. Stir in walnuts. Spread in prepared pan.

Bake 25 to 30 minutes or until wooden pick inserted into center comes out clean. Cool in pan on wire rack. Cut into 2-inch squares. *Makes 16 brownies*

Brownie Kiss Cups

Brownie Kiss Cups

1 package (19.8 ounces) DUNCAN HINES® Chewy Fudge Brownie Mix
1 egg
⅓ cup water
⅓ cup CRISCO® Oil or CRISCO® PURITAN® Canola Oil
25 milk chocolate candy kisses, unwrapped

1. Preheat oven to 350°F. Place 25 (2-inch) foil liners in muffin pans or on cookie sheets.

2. Combine brownie mix, egg, water and oil in large bowl. Stir with spoon until well blended, about 50 strokes. Fill each liner with 2 measuring tablespoonfuls batter. Bake at 350°F for 17 to 20 minutes. Remove from oven. Place 1 milk chocolate candy kiss on each cupcake. Bake 1 minute longer. Cool 5 to 10 minutes in pans. Remove to cooling racks. Cool completely. *Makes 25 brownie cups*

BAKING SECRET

For easy removal of brownies and bar cookies (and no cleanup!), line the baking pan with foil and leave at least 3 inches hanging over on each end. Place the brownies or bars on a cutting board, remove the foil and cut the treats into pieces.

❖

Nutty Chocolate Caramel Bars

2⅓ cups all-purpose flour, divided
2 cups rolled oats
1 cup firmly packed brown sugar
1 teaspoon baking soda
¼ teaspoon salt
1 cup butter or margarine, melted
2 cups (12-ounce package) semi-sweet chocolate pieces
1½ cups chopped DIAMOND® Walnuts
1 (12.25-ounce jar) caramel ice cream topping

Heat oven to 350°F. Combine **2 cups** flour, oats, brown sugar, baking soda and salt. Stir in butter; mix well. Reserve **1 cup** crumb mixture; press remainder into ungreased 13×9-inch pan. Bake at 350°F. for 15 minutes or until lightly browned. Remove from oven; sprinkle with chocolate and walnuts. Combine caramel topping and remaining ⅓ cup flour; drizzle over chocolate and walnuts. Sprinkle with reserved crumb mixture. Return to oven; bake additional 20 minutes or until lightly browned. Cool completely; cut into bars.

Makes 32 bars

One Bowl™ Brownies

4 squares BAKER'S® Unsweetened Chocolate
¾ cup (1½ sticks) margarine or butter
2 cups sugar
3 eggs
1 teaspoon vanilla
1 cup all-purpose flour
1 cup chopped nuts (optional)

PREHEAT oven to 350°F.

MICROWAVE chocolate and margarine in large microwavable bowl on HIGH 2 minutes or until margarine is melted. **Stir until chocolate is completely melted.**

STIR sugar into melted chocolate mixture. Mix in eggs and vanilla until well blended. Stir in flour and nuts. Spread in greased foil-lined 13×9-inch pan.

BAKE for 30 to 35 minutes or until toothpick inserted into center comes out with fudgy crumbs. **Do not overbake.** Cool in pan; cut into squares.

Makes 24 brownies

Prep time: 10 minutes
Bake time: 30 to 35 minutes

Peanut Butter Swirl Brownies: Prepare One Bowl™ Brownie batter as directed, reserving 1 tablespoon of the margarine and 2 tablespoons of the sugar. Add reserved ingredients to ⅔ cup peanut butter; mix well.

Place spoonfuls of peanut butter mixture over brownie batter. Swirl with knife to marbleize. Bake for 30 to 35 minutes or until toothpick inserted into center comes out with fudgy crumbs. Cool in pan; cut into squares. Makes about 24 brownies.

Prep time: 15 minutes
Bake time: 30 to 35 minutes

Rocky Road Brownies: Prepare One Bowl™ Brownies as directed. Bake for 30 minutes. Immediately sprinkle 2 cups miniature marshmallows, 1 cup BAKER'S® Semi-Sweet Real Chocolate Chips and 1 cup chopped nuts over brownies immediately. Continue baking 3 to 5 minutes or until topping begins to melt together. Cool in pan; cut into squares. Makes about 24 brownies.

Prep time: 15 minutes
Bake time: 35 minutes

Chocolate Raspberry Streusel Squares

1½ cups all-purpose flour
1½ cups QUAKER® Oats (quick or old fashioned, uncooked)
½ cup granulated sugar
½ cup firmly packed brown sugar
1 teaspoon baking powder
¼ teaspoon salt (optional)
1 cup (2 sticks) margarine or butter, chilled and cut into pieces
1 cup raspberry preserves or jam (about 10 ounces)
1 cup (6 ounces) semisweet chocolate pieces
¼ cup chopped almonds
½ cup (3 ounces) semisweet chocolate pieces *or* 1 bar (4 ounces) white chocolate, chopped and melted* (optional)

*To melt chocolate: Place in dry glass measuring cup or microwaveable bowl. Microwave at HIGH 1 to 2 minutes, stirring every 30 seconds until smooth. Or, place in top part of dry double boiler over hot, not boiling, water; stir occasionally until smooth.

Heat oven to 375°F. In large bowl, combine flour, oats, sugars, baking powder and salt. Cut in margarine with pastry blender or two knives until mixture is crumbly. Reserve 1 cup oat mixture for streusel; set

aside. Press remaining oat mixture onto bottom of ungreased 9-inch square baking pan. Bake 10 minutes. Spread preserves over crust; sprinkle evenly with chocolate pieces. Combine reserved oat mixture and almonds; sprinkle over chocolate pieces, patting gently. Bake 30 to 35 minutes or until golden brown. Cool completely. Drizzle with melted chocolate, if desired. Let chocolate set before cutting into bars. Store tightly covered.   *Makes 36 bars*

Peanut Butter Marbled Brownies

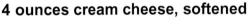

4 ounces cream cheese, softened
½ cup peanut butter
2 tablespoons sugar
1 egg
1 package (20 to 22 ounces) brownie mix plus ingredients to prepare mix
¾ cup lightly salted cocktail peanuts

1. Preheat oven to 350°F. Lightly grease 13×9-inch baking pan; set aside.

2. Beat cream cheese, peanut butter, sugar and egg in medium bowl with electric mixer at medium speed until blended; set aside.

3. Prepare brownie mix according to package directions. Spread evenly in prepared pan. Spoon peanut butter mixture in dollops over brownie mixture. Swirl peanut butter mixture into brownie mixture with tip of knife. Sprinkle peanuts on top; lightly press peanuts down.

4. Bake 30 to 35 minutes or until wooden pick inserted into center comes out almost clean. *Do not overbake.* Cool brownies completely in pan on wire rack. Cut into 2-inch squares.   *Makes 24 brownies*

Replacing the margarine or butter in a recipe with a spread, diet margarine, whipped margarine or whipped butter may result in an inferior baked product. For best results, use the product called for in the recipe.

Orange Coconut Cream Bars

1 18¼-ounce package yellow cake mix
1 cup quick-cooking or old-fashioned oats, uncooked
¾ cup chopped nuts
½ cup butter or margarine, melted
1 large egg
1 14-ounce can sweetened condensed milk
2 teaspoons grated orange zest
1 cup shredded coconut
1 cup "M & M's"® Semi-Sweet Chocolate Mini Baking Bits

Preheat oven to 375°F. Lightly grease 13×9×2-inch baking pan; set aside. In large bowl combine cake mix, oats, nuts, butter and egg until ingredients are thoroughly moistened and mixture resembles coarse crumbs. Reserve 1 cup mixture. Firmly press remaining mixture onto bottom of prepared pan; bake 10 minutes. In separate bowl combine condensed milk and orange zest; spread over baked base. Combine reserved crumb mixture, coconut and "M & M's"® Semi-Sweet Chocolate Mini Baking Bits; sprinkle evenly over condensed milk

mixture and press in lightly. Continue baking 20 to 25 minutes or until golden brown. Cool completely. Cut into bars. Store in tightly covered container.

Makes 26 bars

Praline Bars

¾ cup (1½ sticks) butter or margarine, softened
1 cup sugar, divided
1 teaspoon vanilla, divided
1½ cups flour
2 packages (8 ounces each) PHILADELPHIA BRAND® Cream Cheese, softened
2 eggs
½ cup almond brickle chips
3 tablespoons caramel ice cream topping

MIX butter, ½ cup of the sugar and ½ teaspoon of the vanilla with electric mixer on medium speed until light and fluffy. Gradually add flour, mixing on low speed until blended. Press onto bottom of 13×9-inch baking pan. Bake at 350°F for 20 to 23 minutes or until lightly browned.

MIX cream cheese, remaining ½ cup sugar and ½ teaspoon vanilla with electric mixer on medium speed until well blended. Add eggs; mix well. Blend in chips. Pour over crust. Dot top of cream cheese mixture with topping. Cut through batter with knife several times for marble effect.

BAKE at 350°F for 30 minutes. Cool in pan on wire rack. Refrigerate. Cut into bars. *Makes 24 bars*

Prep time: 30 minutes
Bake time: 30 minutes

Orange Coconut Cream Bars

Brownie Caramel Pecan Bars

½ cup sugar
2 tablespoons butter or margarine
2 tablespoons water
2 cups (12-ounce package)
HERSHEY'S® Semi-Sweet
Chocolate Chips, divided
2 eggs
1 teaspoon vanilla extract
⅔ cup all-purpose flour
¼ teaspoon baking soda
¼ teaspoon salt
Caramel Topping (recipe follows)
1 cup pecan pieces

1. Heat oven to 350°F. Line 9-inch square baking pan with foil, extending foil over edges of pan. Grease and flour foil.

2. In medium saucepan, combine sugar, butter and water; cook over low heat, stirring constantly, until mixture boils. Remove from heat. Immediately add 1 cup chocolate chips; stir until melted. Beat in eggs and vanilla until well blended. Stir together flour, baking soda and salt; stir into chocolate mixture. Spread batter into prepared pan.

3. Bake 15 to 20 minutes or until brownies begin to pull away from sides of pan. Meanwhile, prepare Caramel Topping. Remove brownies from oven; immediately and carefully spread with prepared topping. Sprinkle remaining 1 cup chips and pecans over topping. Cool completely in pan on wire rack, being careful not to disturb chips while soft. Lift out of pan. Cut into bars. *Makes about 16 bars*

Caramel Topping: Remove wrappers from 25 caramels. In medium microwave-safe bowl, place ¼ cup (½ stick) butter or margarine, caramels and 2 tablespoons milk. Microwave at HIGH (100%) 1 minute; stir. Microwave an additional 1 to 2 minutes, stirring every 30 seconds, or until caramels are melted and mixture is smooth when stirred. Use immediately.

Double Decadence Chocolate Chip Brownies

1 cup granulated sugar
⅔ cup (1 stick and 3 tablespoons)
margarine or butter, softened
2 eggs
1 teaspoon vanilla
2 cups (12-ounce package) semi-
sweet chocolate pieces, divided
1¼ cups all-purpose flour
1 cup QUAKER® Oats (quick or old
fashioned, uncooked)
1 teaspoon baking powder
½ cup chopped nuts (optional)
Powdered sugar

HEAT oven to 350°F. **LIGHTLY** grease 13×9-inch baking pan. **BEAT** sugar, margarine, eggs and vanilla until smooth. **ADD** 1 cup chocolate, melted;* mix well. **ADD** flour, oats, baking powder, remaining 1 cup chocolate pieces and nuts, mixing well. **SPREAD** into prepared pan. **BAKE** 25 to 30 minutes or until brownies pull away from sides of pan. **COOL** completely. Sprinkle with powdered sugar, if desired. Cut into bars. *Makes 24 brownies*

*To melt 1 cup chocolate pieces: Microwave at HIGH 1 to 2 minutes, stirring every 30 seconds until smooth. Or, heat in heavy saucepan over low heat, stirring until smooth.

Brownie Caramel Pecan Bars

Mini Kisses® Praline Bars

2 cups all-purpose flour
1⅓ cups packed light brown sugar, divided
½ cup (1 stick) **plus ⅔ cup** butter, divided
1 cup coarsely chopped pecans
1¾ cups (10-ounce package) HERSHEY'S® MINI KISSES® Chocolate

1. Heat oven to 350°F.

2. In large bowl, stir together flour and 1 cup brown sugar; cut in ½ cup butter with pastry blender until fine crumbs form. Press mixture into 13×9×2-inch baking pan; sprinkle with pecans.

3. In small saucepan, place remaining ⅔ cup butter and remaining ⅓ cup brown sugar; cook over medium heat, stirring constantly, until mixture boils. Continue boiling, stirring constantly, 30 seconds, until sugar dissolves; drizzle evenly over pecans and crust.

4. Bake 18 to 22 minutes until topping is bubbly and golden; remove from oven. Immediately sprinkle Mini Kisses Chocolate over top. Cool completely in pan on wire rack. Cut into bars.

Makes about 36 bars

Mini Kisses® Praline Bars

BAKING SECRET

Toasting nuts enhances their flavor. Simply spread nuts in a single layer on a jelly-roll pan and bake in a preheated 325°F oven for 8 to 10 minutes or until lightly toasted, stirring several times. Cool the nuts before using them.

Almond Toffee Bars

¾ cup plus 1 tablespoon butter, softened and divided
¾ cup firmly packed brown sugar
1 egg yolk
½ teaspoon almond extract
½ teaspoon vanilla extract
1½ cups all-purpose flour
¼ teaspoon salt
1 package (12 ounces) semi-sweet chocolate chips
¾ cup BLUE DIAMOND® Chopped Natural Almonds, toasted

Cream ¾ cup butter and sugar; beat in egg yolk and extracts, mixing well. Blend in flour and salt. Spread dough evenly onto bottom of ungreased 13×9×2-inch baking pan. Bake at 350°F. for 25 minutes or until golden brown. Melt chocolate in double boiler over simmering water. Remove from heat and add remaining 1 tablespoon butter. Beat until chocolate is glossy. Spread over baked crust and sprinkle with almonds. Cool to allow chocolate to set. Cut into bars.   *Makes about 35 bars*

Pecan Pie Bars

¾ cup butter or margarine
½ cup powdered sugar
1½ cups all-purpose flour
3 eggs
2 cups coarsely chopped pecans
1 cup granulated sugar
1 cup light corn syrup
2 tablespoons butter or margarine, melted
1 teaspoon vanilla

1. Preheat oven to 350°F.

2. For crust, beat ¾ cup butter in large bowl with electric mixer at medium speed until smooth. Add powdered sugar; beat until well blended. Add flour gradually, beating at low speed after each addition. (Mixture will be crumbly but will press together easily.)

3. Press dough evenly into *ungreased* 13×9-inch baking pan. Press mixture slightly up sides of pan (less than ¼ inch) to form lip to hold filling. Bake 20 to 25 minutes or until golden brown.

4. Meanwhile, for filling, beat eggs lightly in medium bowl with fork. Add pecans, granulated sugar, corn syrup, melted butter and vanilla; mix well. Pour filling over partially baked crust.

5. Return to oven; bake 35 to 40 minutes or until filling is set. Loosen edges with knife. Cool completely on wire rack before cutting into squares. Cover and refrigerate until 10 to 15 minutes before serving time. *Do not freeze.*   *Makes about 48 bars*

Currant Cheesecake Bars

½ **cup butter or margarine, softened**
1 **cup all-purpose flour**
½ **cup packed light brown sugar**
½ **cup finely chopped pecans**
1 **package (8 ounces) cream cheese, softened**
¼ **cup granulated sugar**
1 **egg**
1 **tablespoon milk**
2 **teaspoons grated lemon peel**
⅓ **cup currant jelly or seedless raspberry jam**

1. Preheat oven to 350°F. Grease 9-inch square baking pan. Beat butter in medium bowl with electric mixer at medium speed until smooth. Add flour, brown sugar and pecans; beat at low speed until well blended. Press mixture into bottom and partially up sides of prepared pan.

2. Bake about 15 minutes or until light brown. If sides of crust have shrunk down, press back up and reshape with spoon. Cool 5 minutes on wire rack.

3. Meanwhile, beat cream cheese in large bowl with electric mixer at medium speed until smooth. Add granulated sugar, egg, milk and lemon peel; beat until well blended.

4. Heat jelly in small saucepan over low heat 2 to 3 minutes or until smooth, stirring occasionally.

5. Pour cream cheese mixture over crust. Drizzle jelly in 7 to 8 strips across filling with spoon. Swirl jelly through filling with knife to create marbled effect.

6. Return pan to oven; bake 20 to 25 minutes or until filling is set. Cool completely on wire rack before cutting into bars. Store in airtight container in refrigerator up to 1 week.

Makes about 32 bars

BAKING SECRET

When melting chocolate, avoid high heat because chocolate scorches easily.

Fudgy Chocolate Mint Oatmeal Squares

1¼ **cups all-purpose flour**
½ **teaspoon baking soda**
1 **cup packed brown sugar**
½ **cup (1 stick) butter or margarine, softened**
1 **egg**
1½ **cups quick or old-fashioned oats**
1 **cup chopped nuts**
1½ **cups (10-ounce package) NESTLÉ® TOLL HOUSE® Mint-Chocolate Morsels**
1¼ **cups (14-ounce can) CARNATION® Sweetened Condensed Milk**
2 **tablespoons butter or margarine**

COMBINE flour and baking soda in small bowl. Beat sugar and ½ *cup* butter in large mixer bowl until creamy. Beat in egg. Gradually beat in flour mixture. Stir in oats and nuts. Press *2 cups* oat mixture onto bottom of greased 13×9-inch baking pan.

MELT morsels, sweetened condensed milk and *2 tablespoons* butter in heavy saucepan over low heat, stirring constantly until smooth; pour over crust. Crumble *remaining* oat mixture over filling.

BAKE in preheated 350°F. oven for 25 to 30 minutes or until filling is set and topping begins to brown. Cool in pan on wire rack.

Makes about 30 squares

Currant Cheesecake Bars

Kid-Pleasing Cookies

Remember Mom's cookie jar? Always nestled in its own spot in the kitchen, the cookie jar overflowed with your favorite treats. Continue that never-forgotten tradition for your children and their friends with this selection of kid-pleasing cookies.

Original Nestlé® Toll House® Chocolate Chip Cookies

2¼ cups all-purpose flour
1 teaspoon baking soda
1 teaspoon salt
1 cup (2 sticks) butter, softened
¾ cup granulated sugar
¾ cup packed brown sugar
1 teaspoon vanilla extract
2 eggs
2 cups (12-ounce package) NESTLÉ® TOLL HOUSE® Semi-Sweet Chocolate Morsels
1 cup chopped nuts

COMBINE flour, baking soda and salt in small bowl; set aside.

BEAT butter, granulated sugar, brown sugar and vanilla extract in large bowl until creamy. Beat in eggs. Gradually beat in flour mixture. Stir in morsels and nuts.

Drop by rounded measuring tablespoonfuls onto ungreased cookie sheets.

BAKE in preheated 375°F. oven 9 to 11 minutes or until edges are golden brown. Cool on cookie sheets for 2 minutes. Remove from cookie sheets; cool completely on wire racks.

Makes about 5 dozen cookies

Pan Cookies: PREPARE dough as directed above. Spread dough in greased 15½×10½×1-inch jelly-roll pan. Bake in preheated 375°F. oven for 20 to 25 minutes. Cool completely in pan on wire rack. Cut into 2-inch squares. Makes about 35 squares.

**Original Nestlé® Toll House®
Chocolate Chip Cookies**

52

Black and White Cut-Outs

1 cup butter or margarine, softened
¾ cup granulated sugar
¾ cup packed light brown sugar
2 eggs
1 teaspoon vanilla
2¾ cups plus 2 tablespoons
 all-purpose flour, divided
1 teaspoon baking soda
¾ teaspoon salt
¼ cup unsweetened cocoa powder
1 white baking bar (4 ounces),
 broken into ½-inch pieces
4 ounces semisweet chocolate
 chips
 Assorted decorative candies
 (optional)

Beat butter, granulated sugar and brown sugar in large bowl until light and fluffy. Beat in eggs, 1 at a time. Beat in vanilla. Combine 2¾ cups flour, baking soda and salt in medium bowl; add to butter mixture. Beat until well blended. Remove half of dough from bowl; reserve. To make chocolate dough, beat cocoa into remaining dough with spoon until well blended. To make butter cookie dough, beat remaining 2 tablespoons flour into reserved dough. Flatten each half of dough into a disc; wrap in plastic wrap and refrigerate about 1½ hours or until firm.

Preheat oven to 375°F. Working with one dough at a time, place on lightly floured surface. Roll out dough to ¼-inch thickness. Cut into desired shapes with cookie cutters. Place cookies 1 inch apart on ungreased cookie sheets. Bake 9 to 11 minutes or until set. Let cookies stand on cookie sheets 2 minutes. Remove cookies to wire racks; cool completely.

For white chocolate drizzle, place baking bar pieces in small heavy resealable plastic bag; seal bag. Microwave at

MEDIUM (50% power) 2 minutes. Turn bag over; heat at MEDIUM 2 to 3 minutes or until melted. Knead bag until white chocolate is smooth. Cut small corner from bag; pipe or drizzle melted chocolate onto chocolate cookies. Decorate as desired with assorted candies. Let stand until white chocolate is set, about 30 minutes.

For chocolate drizzle, place chocolate chips in small heavy resealable plastic bag; seal bag. Microwave at HIGH 1 minute. Turn bag over; heat at HIGH 1 to 2 minutes or until chocolate is melted. Knead bag until chocolate is smooth. Cut small corner from bag; pipe or drizzle chocolate onto butter cookies. Decorate as desired with assorted candies. Let stand until chocolate is set, about 40 minutes.

Makes 3 to 4 dozen cookies

Black and White Sandwiches: Cut cookies out with cookie cutter. Bake according to above directions. Spread thin layer of prepared frosting on bottom side of chocolate cookie. Place bottom side of butter cookie over frosting. Drizzle either side of cookie with melted chocolate or white chocolate.

BAKING SECRET

For easy cleanup when rolling cookie dough, roll out the dough on a sheet of waxed paper that has been placed right on the countertop. To prevent the waxed paper from sliding, lightly spray the countertop under it with water.

Maple Walnut Cookies

Maple Walnut Cookies

❀ ─────────────────── ❀

1¼ cups firmly packed light brown
      sugar
¾ Butter Flavor CRISCO® Stick or
      ¾ cup Butter Flavor CRISCO®
      all-vegetable shortening
2 tablespoons maple syrup
1 teaspoon vanilla
1 teaspoon maple extract
1 egg
1¾ cups all-purpose flour
1 teaspoon salt
¾ teaspoon baking soda
½ teaspoon cinnamon
1½ cups chopped walnuts
30 to 40 walnut halves

1. Heat oven to 375°F. Place sheets of foil on countertop for cooling cookies.

2. Place brown sugar, shortening, maple syrup, vanilla and maple extract in large bowl. Beat at medium speed of electric mixer until well blended. Add egg; beat well.

3. Combine flour, salt, baking soda and cinnamon. Add to shortening mixture; beat at low speed just until blended. Stir in chopped walnuts.

4. Drop dough by rounded measuring tablespoonfuls 3 inches apart onto ungreased cookie sheets. Press walnut half into center of each cookie.

5. Bake one cookie sheet at a time at 375°F for 8 to 10 minutes for chewy cookies, or 11 to 13 minutes for crisp cookies. *Do not overbake.* Cool 2 minutes on baking sheet. Remove cookies to foil to cool completely.

Makes about 3 dozen cookies

Moravian Spice Crisps

⅓ cup shortening
⅓ cup packed brown sugar
¼ cup unsulfured molasses
¼ cup dark corn syrup
1¾ to 2 cups all-purpose flour, divided
2 teaspoons ground ginger
1¼ teaspoons baking soda
1 teaspoon ground cinnamon
½ teaspoon ground cloves
Powdered sugar

1. Melt shortening in small saucepan over low heat. Remove from heat; stir in brown sugar, molasses and corn syrup. Cool.

2. Combine 1½ cups flour, ginger, baking soda, cinnamon and cloves in large bowl. Beat in shortening mixture with electric mixer at medium speed. Beat in additional flour until stiff dough forms.

3. Knead dough on lightly floured surface, adding more flour if too sticky. Form dough into 2 discs; wrap in plastic wrap and refrigerate 30 minutes or until firm.

4. Preheat oven to 350°F. Grease cookie sheets; set aside. Working with 1 disc at a time, unwrap dough and place on lightly floured surface. Roll out dough with lightly floured rolling pin to 1/16-inch thickness.

5. Cut dough with floured 2⅜-inch scalloped cookie cutter. (If dough becomes too soft, refrigerate several minutes before continuing.) Gently press dough trimmings together; reroll and cut out more cookies. Place cookies ½ inch apart on prepared cookie sheets.

6. Bake 8 minutes or until firm. Remove cookies to wire racks; cool completely.

7. Place small strips of cardboard or parchment paper over cookies; dust with sifted powdered sugar. Carefully remove cardboard.

Makes about 6 dozen cookies

BAKING SECRET

Never store two kinds of cookies in the same container, because their flavors and textures can change.

❈

Soft Spicy Molasses Cookies

2 cups all-purpose flour
1 cup sugar
¾ cup margarine or butter, softened
⅓ cup light molasses
3 tablespoons milk
1 egg
½ teaspoon baking soda
½ teaspoon ground ginger
½ teaspoon ground cinnamon
½ teaspoon ground cloves
⅛ teaspoon salt
Sugar for rolling

Combine flour, 1 cup sugar, margarine, molasses, milk, egg, baking soda, ginger, cinnamon, cloves and salt in large bowl. Beat at low speed of electric mixer, 2 to 3 minutes. Cover; refrigerate until firm enough to handle, at least 4 hours or overnight.

Preheat oven to 350°F. Shape dough into 1-inch balls; roll in sugar. Place 2 inches apart on ungreased cookie sheets. Bake 9 to 12 minutes or until just firm to the touch. Remove immediately to wire racks to cool.   *Makes about 4 dozen cookies*

Moravian Spice Crisps

Peanut Butter Thumbprints
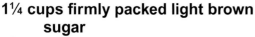

1¼ cups firmly packed light brown sugar
¾ cup creamy peanut butter
½ CRISCO® Stick or ½ cup CRISCO® all-vegetable shortening
3 tablespoons milk
1 tablespoon vanilla
1 egg
1¾ cups all-purpose flour
¾ teaspoon baking soda
¾ teaspoon salt
  Granulated sugar
¼ cup strawberry jam,* stirred

*Substitute your favorite jam or jelly for strawberry jam.

1. Heat oven to 375°F. Place sheets of foil on countertop for cooling cookies.

2. Place brown sugar, peanut butter, shortening, milk and vanilla in large bowl. Beat at medium speed of electric mixer until well blended. Add egg; beat just until blended.

3. Combine flour, baking soda and salt. Add to shortening mixture; beat at low speed just until blended.

4. Shape dough into 1-inch balls. Roll in granulated sugar. Place 2 inches apart on ungreased cookie sheets.

5. Bake one cookie sheet at a time at 375°F for 6 minutes. Press centers of cookies immediately with back of measuring teaspoon. Bake 3 minutes longer or until cookies are set and just beginning to brown. *Do not overbake.* Cool 2 minutes on baking sheet. Spoon jam into center of each cookie. Remove cookies to foil to cool completely.

Makes about 4 dozen cookies

Crispy Oat Drops
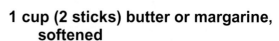

1 cup (2 sticks) butter or margarine, softened
½ cup granulated sugar
½ cup firmly packed light brown sugar
1 large egg
2 cups all-purpose flour
½ cup quick-cooking or old-fashioned oats, uncooked
1 teaspoon cream of tartar
½ teaspoon baking soda
¼ teaspoon salt
1¾ cups "M & M's"® Semi-Sweet Chocolate Mini Baking Bits
1 cup toasted rice cereal
½ cup shredded coconut
½ cup coarsely chopped pecans

Preheat oven to 350°F. In large bowl cream butter and sugars until light and fluffy; beat in egg. In medium bowl combine flour, oats, cream of tartar, baking soda and salt; blend flour mixture into creamed mixture. Stir in "M & M's"® Semi-Sweet Chocolate Mini Baking Bits, cereal, coconut and pecans. Drop by heaping tablespoonfuls about 2 inches apart onto ungreased cookie sheets. Bake 10 to 13 minutes or until lightly browned. Cool completely on wire racks. Store in tightly covered container.

Makes about 4 dozen cookies

 BAKING SECRET

For more uniformly shaped drop cookies, scoop dough using a small ice cream scoop with a release bar. The handiest sizes are 40, 50 and 80.

Molded Scotch Shortbread

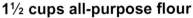

1½ **cups all-purpose flour**
¼ **teaspoon salt**
¾ **cup butter, softened**
⅓ **cup sugar**
1 **large egg**
  10-inch diameter ceramic shortbread mold

1. Preheat oven to temperature recommended by shortbread mold manufacturer. Place flour and salt in medium bowl; stir to combine.

2. Beat butter and sugar in large bowl with electric mixer at medium speed until light and fluffy. Beat in egg. Gradually add flour mixture. Beat at low speed until well blended.

3. Spray shortbread mold with nonstick cooking spray. Press dough firmly into mold. Bake, cool and remove from mold according to manufacturer's directions.

4. If mold is not available, preheat oven to 350°F. Roll tablespoonfuls of dough into 1-inch balls. Place balls 2 inches apart on *ungreased* cookie sheet; press with fork to flatten.

5. Bake 18 to 20 minutes or until edges are lightly browned. Let cookies stand on cookie sheet 2 minutes. Remove cookies with spatula to wire rack; cool completely.

6. Store cookies tightly covered at room temperature or freeze up to 3 months.

Makes 1 shortbread mold or 2 dozen cookies

BAKING SECRET

When reusing cookie sheets for several batches of cookies, cool the sheets completely before placing dough on them. The dough will soften and begin to spread on a hot baking sheet.

Fudgy Peanut Butter Jiffy Cookies

2 **cups granulated sugar**
½ **cup evaporated milk**
½ **cup (1 stick) margarine or butter**
¼ **cup unsweetened cocoa powder**
2½ **cups QUAKER® Oats (quick or old fashioned, uncooked)**
½ **cup peanut butter**
½ **cup raisins or chopped dates**
2 **teaspoons vanilla**

In large saucepan, combine sugar, milk, margarine and cocoa. Bring to a boil over medium heat, stirring frequently. Continue boiling 3 minutes. Remove from heat. Stir in oats, peanut butter, raisins and vanilla; mix well. Quickly drop by tablespoonfuls onto waxed paper or greased cookie sheet. Let stand until set. Store tightly covered at room temperature.

Makes about 3 dozen cookies

Double-Dipped Chocolate Peanut Butter Cookies

1¼ cups all-purpose flour
½ teaspoon baking powder
½ teaspoon baking soda
½ teaspoon salt
½ cup butter or margarine, softened
  Granulated sugar
½ cup packed light brown sugar
½ cup creamy or chunky peanut
  butter
1 egg
1 teaspoon vanilla
1½ cups semisweet chocolate chips
3 teaspoons shortening, divided
1½ cups milk chocolate chips

PREHEAT oven to 350°F. Combine flour, baking powder, baking soda and salt in small bowl.

BEAT butter, ½ cup granulated sugar and brown sugar in large bowl with electric mixer at medium speed until light and fluffy. Beat in peanut butter, egg and vanilla. Gradually stir in flour mixture until blended.

SHAPE heaping tablespoonfuls of dough into 1½-inch balls. Place balls 2 inches apart on *ungreased* cookie sheets. (If dough is too soft, refrigerate 30 minutes.)

DIP table fork into granulated sugar; press criss-cross fashion onto each ball, flattening to ½-inch thickness.

BAKE 12 minutes or until set. Let cookies stand on cookie sheets 2 minutes; transfer to wire racks to cool completely.

MELT semisweet chocolate chips and 1½ teaspoons shortening in heavy small saucepan over low heat. Dip one end of each cookie in mixture; place on waxed paper. Let stand until chocolate is set,

about 30 minutes. Repeat with milk chocolate chips and remaining 1½ teaspoons shortening, dipping opposite ends of cookies. Store cookies between sheets of waxed paper in cool place or freeze up to 3 months.
Makes about 24 (3-inch) cookies

Peanut Butter Delights

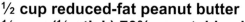

½ cup reduced-fat peanut butter
¼ cup (½ stick) 70% vegetable oil
  spread, softened
½ cup firmly packed brown sugar
½ cup unsweetened applesauce
2 egg whites
½ teaspoon vanilla
1 cup all-purpose flour
½ cup KRETSCHMER® Wheat Germ,
  any flavor
1 teaspoon baking soda
¼ teaspoon salt (optional)
¼ cup miniature semisweet
  chocolate morsels

Heat oven to 350°F. In large bowl, beat peanut butter and vegetable oil spread on medium speed of electric mixer until creamy. Add sugar; beat well. Add applesauce, egg whites and vanilla; beat well. Add combined flour, wheat germ, baking soda and salt; mix well. Stir in chocolate morsels. Drop by tablespoonfuls onto ungreased cookie sheets. Sprinkle with additional wheat germ, if desired. Bake 10 to 12 minutes or just until cookies are set. *(Do not overbake.)* Cool 1 minute on cookie sheets; remove to wire rack. Cool completely. Store tightly covered.
Makes 2½ dozen cookies

**Double-Dipped Chocolate
Peanut Butter Cookies**

Quick Chocolate Softies

1 package (18.25 ounces) devil's food cake mix
⅓ cup water
¼ cup butter or margarine, softened
1 egg
1 cup white chocolate baking chips
½ cup coarsely chopped walnuts

Preheat oven to 350°F. Grease cookie sheets. Combine cake mix, water, butter and egg in large bowl. Beat with electric mixer at low speed until moistened. Increase speed to medium; beat 1 minute. (Dough will be thick.) Stir in chips and nuts; mix until well blended. Drop dough by heaping teaspoonfuls 2 inches apart onto prepared cookie sheets.

Bake 10 to 12 minutes or until set. Let cookies stand on cookie sheets 1 minute. Remove cookies to wire racks; cool completely.

Makes about 4 dozen cookies

BAKING SECRET

Grease cookie sheets only if directed to do so in the recipe. Some cookie doughs are high enough in fat that they will not stick to the sheet.

Bananaramas

1¼ cups firmly packed light brown sugar
¾ cup creamy peanut butter
½ CRISCO® Stick or ½ cup CRISCO® all-vegetable shortening
1 cup mashed banana
3 tablespoons milk
1½ teaspoons vanilla
½ teaspoon almond extract
1 egg
2 cups all-purpose flour
¾ teaspoon baking soda
¾ teaspoon salt
1½ cups milk chocolate chunks or semisweet chocolate chunks*
1 cup peanuts or coarsely chopped pecans (optional)

*A combination of milk chocolate and semisweet chocolate chunks can be used.

1. Heat oven to 350°F. Place sheets of foil on countertop for cooling cookies.

2. Place brown sugar, peanut butter, shortening, banana, milk, vanilla and almond extract in large bowl. Beat at medium speed of electric mixer until well blended. Add egg; beat just until blended.

3. Combine flour, baking soda and salt. Add to shortening mixture; beat at low speed just until blended. Stir in chocolate chunks and nuts, if desired.

4. Drop dough by rounded measuring tablespoonfuls 2 inches apart onto ungreased cookie sheets.

5. Bake one cookie sheet at a time at 350°F for 11 to 13 minutes or until cookies are light brown around edges. *Do not overbake.* Cool 2 minutes on cookie sheet. Remove cookies to foil to cool completely.

Makes about 4 dozen cookies

Chewy Oatmeal Cookies

1¼ cups firmly packed light brown
 sugar
¾ Butter Flavor CRISCO® Stick or
 ¾ cup Butter Flavor CRISCO®
 all-vegetable shortening
1 egg
⅓ cup milk
1½ teaspoons vanilla
3 cups quick oats, uncooked
1 cup all-purpose flour
½ teaspoon baking soda
½ teaspoon salt
¼ teaspoon cinnamon
1 cup raisins
1 cup coarsely chopped walnuts

1. Heat oven to 375°F. Grease cookie sheets. Place sheets of foil on countertop for cooling cookies.

2. Place brown sugar, shortening, egg, milk and vanilla in large bowl. Beat at medium speed of electric mixer until well blended.

3. Combine oats, flour, baking soda, salt and cinnamon. Add to shortening mixture; beat at low speed just until blended. Stir in raisins and walnuts.

4. Drop dough by rounded measuring tablespoonfuls 2 inches apart onto prepared cookie sheets.

5. Bake one cookie sheet at a time at 375°F for 10 to 12 minutes or until cookies are lightly browned. *Do not overbake.* Cool 2 minutes on baking sheet. Remove cookies to foil to cool completely.
Makes about 2½ dozen cookies

Nutty Clusters

4 squares (1 ounce each)
 unsweetened chocolate, divided
1 cup granulated sugar
½ cup plus 2 tablespoons butter or
 margarine, softened, divided
1 egg
⅓ cup buttermilk
1 teaspoon vanilla
1¾ cups all-purpose flour
½ teaspoon baking soda
1 cup mixed salted nuts, coarsely
 chopped
2 cups powdered sugar
2 to 3 tablespoons water

For cookies: **PREHEAT** oven to 400°F. Line cookie sheets with parchment paper or leave ungreased. Melt 2 squares chocolate in heavy small saucepan over very low heat. Remove from heat; let cool.

BEAT granulated sugar and ½ cup butter in large bowl with electric mixer until smooth. Beat in melted chocolate, egg, buttermilk and vanilla until light. Stir in flour and baking soda just until blended. Stir in nuts.

DROP teaspoonfuls of dough 2 inches apart onto prepared cookie sheets.

BAKE 8 to 10 minutes or until almost no imprint remains when touched. Immediately transfer cookies to wire rack.

Meanwhile, for icing, **MELT** remaining 2 squares chocolate and 2 tablespoons butter in small heavy saucepan over low heat, stirring until completely melted. Add powdered sugar and water, mixing until smooth. Frost cookies while still warm.
Makes about 4 dozen cookies

Heartwarming Fruit Desserts

You'll find a great-tasting fruit dessert for every season in this chapter. Try a warm cinnamony baked apple on a crisp fall evening, a satisfying fruity bread pudding to top off a winter dinner, a luscious fresh strawberry shortcake to celebrate spring or a cool succulent berry cobbler to end a hot summer day.

Fresh Berry Cobbler Cake

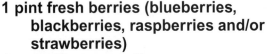

1 pint fresh berries (blueberries, blackberries, raspberries and/or strawberries)
1 cup all-purpose flour
1¼ cups sugar, divided
1 teaspoon baking powder
¼ teaspoon salt
3 tablespoons butter or margarine
½ cup milk
1 tablespoon cornstarch
1 cup cold water
Additional berries (optional)

Preheat oven to 375°F. Place berries in 9-inch square baking pan; set aside. Combine flour, ½ cup sugar, baking powder and salt in large bowl. Cut in butter with pastry blender or two knives until coarse crumbs form. Stir in milk. Spoon over berries. Combine remaining ¾ cup sugar and cornstarch in small bowl. Stir in water until sugar mixture dissolves; pour over berry mixture. Bake 35 to 40 minutes or until lightly browned. Serve warm or cool completely. Garnish with additional berries, if desired. *Makes 6 servings*

Favorite recipe from **Bob Evans Farms**®

BAKING SECRET

Most cobblers and crisps are best served warm or at room temperature the day they are made. Leftovers should be covered and refrigerated.

Fresh Berry Cobbler Cake

Almond-Pear Strudel

5 to 6 cups thinly sliced crisp pears (about 5)
1 tablespoon grated lemon peel
1 tablespoon lemon juice
⅓ cup plus 1 teaspoon sugar, divided
2 teaspoons ground cinnamon
1 teaspoon ground nutmeg
6 sheets (¼ pound) phyllo dough
4 tablespoons melted butter or margarine, divided
½ teaspoon almond extract
¾ cup slivered almonds, toasted, divided
Powdered sugar (optional)

1. Place sliced pears in large microwavable container. Stir in lemon peel and lemon juice. Microwave on HIGH 6 minutes or until tender; cool. Combine ⅓ cup sugar, cinnamon and nutmeg in small bowl. Cover pears and refrigerate.

2. Lay 2 sheets of plastic wrap on work surface to make 20-inch square. Place 1 phyllo sheet in middle of plastic wrap. (Cover remaining dough with damp kitchen towel to prevent drying.) Brush 1 teaspoon melted butter onto phyllo sheet. Place second phyllo sheet over first; brush with 1 teaspoon butter. Repeat layering with remaining sheets of phyllo.

3. Preheat oven to 400°F. Drain pear mixture; toss with sugar mixture and almond extract. Spread pear mixture evenly over phyllo leaving 3-inch strip on far long side. Sprinkle pear mixture with ½ cup toasted almonds. Brush strip with 2 teaspoons melted butter. Beginning at long side of phyllo opposite strip, roll up jelly-roll style, forming strudel. Place seam-side down onto buttered baking sheet. Brush top with 1 teaspoon butter. Bake 20 minutes or until golden. Brush with 1 teaspoon butter. Stir remaining ¼ cup almonds and 1 teaspoon sugar with remaining teaspoons butter; sprinkle on top of strudel. Bake 5 minutes more. Cool 10 minutes; sprinkle with powdered sugar, if desired. *Makes 8 servings*

Note: To make ahead, complete steps 1 and 2. Cover and refrigerate pears overnight. Cover sugar mixture and set aside. Cover phyllo and remaining butter; refrigerate overnight. To complete recipe, proceed with step 3, melting reserved butter before using.

Granny Smith Crisp

5 cups peeled, cored and sliced Granny Smith apples
½ cup sugar
1 teaspoon ground cinnamon
Streusel Topping (recipe follows)

Heat oven to 350°F. In large bowl, toss apples with sugar and cinnamon; spread apple mixture in 11×8-inch baking pan. Prepare Streusel Topping; spread evenly over apples. Bake 35 to 40 minutes or until apples are tender. *Makes 6 servings*

Streusel Topping: In medium bowl, combine ¾ cup all-purpose flour, ¼ cup granulated sugar and ¼ cup packed brown sugar. With pastry blender or 2 knives, cut in ½ cup (1 stick) butter until crumbly mixture is formed. Stir in ½ cup quick rolled oats.

Favorite recipe from **Washington Apple Commission**

Almond-Pear Strudel

Giant Strawberry Shortcake

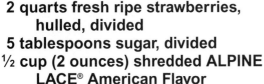

2 quarts fresh ripe strawberries, hulled, divided

5 tablespoons sugar, divided

½ cup (2 ounces) shredded ALPINE LACE® American Flavor Pasteurized Process Cheese Product

2 cups all-purpose flour

1 tablespoon baking powder

1 tablespoon grated lime peel, divided

¾ teaspoon salt

½ teaspoon baking soda

¼ cup unsalted butter, at room temperature

¼ cup vegetable shortening

¾ cup buttermilk

¼ cup egg substitute or 1 large whole egg

¾ cup low fat vanilla yogurt

½ cup fat free sour cream

1. Preheat oven to 450°F. Butter 12-inch fluted tart pan with 1-inch side and removable bottom. Using food processor or blender, purée 1 cup berries and 2 tablespoons of the sugar; pour into serving bowl. Slice remaining berries and toss with purée. Cover; let stand at room temperature.

2. In food processor, process cheese until finely ground. Add flour, 1 tablespoon of the sugar, the baking powder, 2 teaspoons lime peel, salt and baking soda; process 15 seconds. Transfer to a large bowl. Using pastry cutter or 2 knives, cut in butter and shortening until mixture resembles coarse crumbs. In small bowl, whisk buttermilk and egg substitute (or whole egg) and add to flour mixture. Mix just until a soft dough forms. Turn dough onto lightly floured board; knead for about 30 seconds. Pat dough on bottom and side of pan and trim edges to stand 1 inch high. Bake for 11 minutes or just until lightly browned. Let cake cool in pan on rack for 5 minutes.

3. Meanwhile, in small bowl, blend yogurt and sour cream with the remaining 2 tablespoons of sugar and 1 teaspoon of lime peel; refrigerate. To serve, remove side, leaving cake on removable bottom of pan; place on platter. Top with berry mixture and some yogurt-cream. Serve with remaining yogurt-cream.

Makes 12 servings

BAKING SECRET

To reduce the risk of bacterial contamination of eggs, always keep them cold. If a recipe calls for room temperature eggs, let them sit on the counter for 30 minutes or place them in bowl of warm, not hot, water for 10 minutes; then use them immediately.

Giant Strawberry Shortcake

Blueberry Bread Pudding with Caramel Sauce

Blueberry Bread Pudding with Caramel Sauce

8 slices white bread, cubed
1 cup fresh or frozen blueberries
2 cups skim milk
1 cup EGG BEATERS® Healthy Egg Substitute
⅔ cup sugar
1 teaspoon vanilla extract
¼ teaspoon ground cinnamon
   Caramel Sauce (recipe follows)

Place bread cubes in bottom of lightly greased 8×8×2-inch baking pan. Sprinkle with blueberries; set aside.

In large bowl, combine milk, Egg Beaters, sugar, vanilla and cinnamon; pour over bread mixture. Set pan in larger pan filled with 1-inch depth hot water. Bake at 350°F for 1 hour or until knife inserted in center comes out clean. Serve warm with Caramel Sauce.   *Makes 9 servings*

Prep time: 20 minutes
Cook time: 1 hour

CARAMEL SAUCE: In small saucepan, over low heat, heat ¼ cup skim milk and 14 vanilla caramels until caramels are melted, stirring frequently.

Walnut-Raisin Baked Apples

6 large baking apples, such as Rome Beauty
1 cup plus 2 tablespoons packed light brown sugar, divided
1 cup (4 ounces) shredded ALPINE LACE® American Flavor Pasteurized Process Cheese Product
¾ cup golden raisins
⅓ cup chopped California walnuts, toasted
1 teaspoon ground cinnamon
3 tablespoons fresh lemon juice
2 cups apple cider

1. Preheat the oven to 375°F. Spray a shallow baking dish with nonstick cooking spray.

2. Core the apples, cutting almost through, but not through, the bottoms of the apples, leaving about a 2-inch-wide cavity in the centers. Pare apples one third of the way down from the top stem end, then place upright in the baking dish. If necessary, cut a thin slice off the bottoms of the apples so they stand firm.

3. In a small bowl, toss together the 1 cup of brown sugar, the cheese, raisins, walnuts and cinnamon. Using a small spoon, stuff one sixth of the cheese mixture into the cavity of each apple, mounding it in the center. Drizzle the lemon juice over the apples. Pour the cider in the baking dish around the apples.

4. Bake the apples, uncovered, for 35 minutes, basting every 10 minutes with the cider. Sprinkle with the remaining 2 tablespoons sugar and bake 10 minutes more or until the apples can be pierced easily with a fork. To serve, transfer each apple to a serving dish and spoon some of the cider sauce over each serving.

Makes 6 servings

Fresh Nectarine-Pineapple Cobbler

1 DOLE® Fresh Pineapple
3 cups sliced ripe DOLE® Nectarines or Peaches
½ cup sugar
2 tablespoons all-purpose flour
½ teaspoon ground cinnamon
1 cup buttermilk baking mix
½ cup low-fat or nonfat milk

• **Twist** crown from pineapple. Cut pineapple in half lengthwise. Cover and refrigerate one half for another use. Cut remaining pineapple in half lengthwise. Remove fruit from shell; core and chop fruit.

• **Combine** pineapple, nectarines, sugar, flour and cinnamon in large bowl. Spoon into 8-inch square glass baking dish.

• **Stir** baking mix and milk in small bowl until baking mix is just moistened; pour over fruit.

• **Bake** at 400°F 40 to 45 minutes or until fruit is tender and crust is lightly browned.

Makes 8 servings

Prep time: 20 minutes
Bake time: 45 minutes

BAKING SECRET

To hasten ripening of fruit, such as peaches, nectarines, plums and pears, place them in a closed paper bag at room temperature for several days. Store ripe fruit in the refrigerator and use within a few days.

BAKING SECRET

For fruit desserts with the best flavor, use fully ripened fruit.

❈

Berry Cobbler

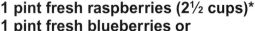

1 pint fresh raspberries (2½ cups)*
1 pint fresh blueberries or
    strawberries, sliced (2½ cups)*
⅓ cup sugar
2 tablespoons cornstarch
1 cup all-purpose flour
1 tablespoon sugar
1½ teaspoons baking powder
¼ teaspoon salt
½ cup milk
⅓ cup butter or margarine, melted
¼ teaspoon ground nutmeg

*One (16-ounce) bag frozen raspberries and one (16-ounce) bag frozen blueberries or strawberries may be substituted for fresh berries. Thaw berries, reserving juices. Increase cornstarch to 3 tablespoons.

Preheat oven to 375°F. Combine berries, ⅓ cup sugar and cornstarch in medium bowl; toss lightly to coat. Spoon into 1½-quart or 8-inch square baking dish. Combine flour, 1 tablespoon sugar, baking powder and salt in medium bowl. Add milk and butter; mix just until dry ingredients are moistened. Drop six heaping tablespoonfuls of batter evenly over berries; sprinkle with nutmeg. Bake 25 minutes or until topping is golden brown and fruit is bubbly. Cool on wire rack. Serve warm or at room temperature.
Makes 6 servings

Cherry-Chocolate Crumble

1½ cups graham cracker crumbs
3 tablespoons sugar
¼ cup Prune Purée (recipe follows)
    or prepared prune butter
¼ cup semisweet miniature
    chocolate chips
2 cans (20 ounces each) cherry pie
    filling

Preheat oven to 375°F. In medium bowl, mix crumbs and sugar. Cut in prune purée with pastry blender until mixture resembles coarse crumbs. Mix in chocolate chips. Spread pie filling evenly in 8-inch square baking dish or pan; cover evenly with crumb mixture. Bake in center of oven about 20 minutes until cherries are bubbly and topping is lightly browned. Cool on wire rack 15 minutes. Serve warm, topped with fat-free vanilla frozen yogurt, if desired.
Makes 8 servings

Prune Purée: Combine 1⅓ cups (8 ounces) pitted prunes and 6 tablespoons hot water in container of food processor or blender. Pulse on and off until prunes are finely chopped and smooth. Store leftovers in covered container in refrigerator for up to two months. Makes 1 cup.

Favorite recipe from **California Prune Board**

Berry Cobbler

Streusel Topped Peach Cobbler

1 can (29 ounces) *or* 2 cans
    (16 ounces each) cling peach
    slices in syrup
⅓ cup plus 1 tablespoon granulated
    sugar, divided
1 tablespoon cornstarch
½ teaspoon vanilla
½ cup packed brown sugar
2 cups all-purpose flour, divided
⅓ cup uncooked quick oats
¼ cup margarine or butter, melted
½ teaspoon ground cinnamon
½ teaspoon salt
½ cup shortening
4 to 5 tablespoons cold water
    Sweetened Whipped Cream
    (recipe follows)

Drain peach slices; reserve ¾ cup syrup. Combine ⅓ cup granulated sugar and cornstarch in small saucepan. Slowly add reserved syrup. Stir well. Cook over low heat, stirring constantly, until thickened. Add vanilla. Set aside.

Combine brown sugar, ½ cup flour, oats, margarine and cinnamon in small bowl; stir until mixture forms coarse crumbs. Set aside.

Preheat oven to 350°F. Combine remaining 1½ cups flour, 1 tablespoon granulated sugar and salt in small bowl. Cut in shortening until mixture forms pea-sized pieces. Sprinkle water, 1 tablespoon at a time, over flour mixture. Toss lightly with fork until mixture holds together. Press together to form a ball.

Press dough between hands to form a 5- to 6-inch disc. Roll dough into square, ⅛ inch thick, on lightly floured surface. Cut into 10-inch square. Press dough onto bottom and 1 inch up sides of 8-inch square baking dish.

Arrange peaches over crust. Pour sauce over peaches. Sprinkle with crumb topping. Bake 45 minutes. Prepare Sweetened Whipped Cream. Serve cobbler warm or at room temperature with Sweetened Whipped Cream.

Makes about 6 servings

Sweetened Whipped Cream

1 cup whipping cream, chilled
3 tablespoons sugar
½ teaspoon vanilla

Chill large bowl and beaters thoroughly. Pour chilled whipping cream into bowl and beat with electric mixer at high speed until soft peaks form. Gradually add sugar and vanilla. Whip until stiff peaks form.

Apple Crisp

5 cups peeled and sliced apples
½ cup raisins
1 cup all-purpose flour
½ cup sugar
½ teaspoon baking powder
½ teaspoon salt
1 egg
⅓ cup butter or margarine, melted
    Ground cinnamon to taste
    Vanilla ice cream (optional)

Preheat oven to 350°F. Combine apples and raisins in 8-inch square baking pan. Combine flour, sugar, baking powder and salt. Stir in egg with fork until crumbly. Sprinkle over apple mixture. Drizzle with butter and sprinkle with cinnamon. Bake 30 minutes or until lightly browned and apples are tender. Serve warm with vanilla ice cream, if desired. Refrigerate leftovers.

Makes 9 servings

Favorite recipe from **Bob Evans Farms**

Streusel Topped Peach Cobbler

Country Breads

Warm breads on beautiful country mornings—what a wonderful memory! Even if you can't get to the country now, your family can enjoy cozy times at home in a kitchen filled with the aromas of freshly baked breads.

Orange-Currant Scones

1½ cups all-purpose flour
¼ cup plus 1 teaspoon sugar, divided
1 teaspoon baking powder
¼ teaspoon salt
¼ teaspoon baking soda
⅓ cup currants
1 tablespoon grated orange peel
6 tablespoons chilled butter or margarine, cut into small pieces
½ cup buttermilk, plain yogurt, or regular or nonfat sour cream

1. Preheat oven to 425°F.

2. Combine flour, ¼ cup sugar, baking powder, salt and baking soda in large bowl. Stir in currants and orange peel.

3. Cut in butter with pastry blender or 2 knives until mixture resembles coarse crumbs.

4. Stir in buttermilk. Stir until mixture forms soft dough that clings together. (Dough will be sticky.)

5. Lightly flour hands and shape dough into a ball. Pat dough into 8-inch round on lightly greased baking sheet. Cut dough into 8 wedges with floured chef's knife.

6. Sprinkle wedges with remaining 1 teaspoon sugar. Bake 18 to 20 minutes or until lightly browned.

Makes 8 scones

BAKING SECRET

To test if a yeast dough has risen properly, lightly press two fingertips about one-half inch into the dough. The dough is ready if an indentation remains when fingertips are removed.

Cinnamon-Raisin Bread

1 package active dry yeast
½ cup plus 1 teaspoon sugar, divided
¼ cup warm water (105° to 115°F)
2 eggs
3 to 3½ cups all-purpose flour, divided
1 teaspoon salt
⅔ cup warm milk (105° to 115°F)
3 tablespoons butter or margarine, softened
1 teaspoon vanilla
¾ cup raisins
1 tablespoon ground cinnamon
1 tablespoon butter or margarine, melted
1 tablespoon water

To proof yeast, sprinkle yeast and 1 teaspoon sugar over warm water in small bowl; stir until yeast is dissolved. Let stand 5 minutes or until mixture is bubbly. Separate 1 egg. Place yolk in another bowl; set aside. Cover white and reserve in refrigerator.

Combine 1½ cups flour, ¼ cup sugar and salt in large bowl. Gradually beat yeast mixture, warm milk and softened butter into flour mixture with electric mixer at low speed. Increase speed to medium; beat 2 minutes. Reduce speed to low. Beat in remaining whole egg, egg yolk and vanilla. Increase speed to medium; beat 2 minutes. Stir in raisins and enough additional flour, about 1½ cups, to make soft dough. Turn out dough onto lightly floured surface; flatten slightly. Knead dough about 5 minutes or until smooth and elastic, adding ½ cup more flour to prevent sticking, if necessary. (Dough will be soft and slightly sticky.)

Shape dough into ball; place in large greased bowl. Turn dough over so that top is greased. Cover with towel; let rise in warm place 1 to 1½ hours or until doubled in bulk. Punch down dough. Knead dough on lightly floured surface 1 minute. Cover with towel; let rest 10 minutes. Grease 9×5-inch loaf pan; set aside. Combine remaining ¼ cup sugar and cinnamon. Place 1 tablespoon mixture in small cup; reserve.

Roll dough into 20×9-inch rectangle with lightly floured rolling pin. Brush with 1 tablespoon melted butter. Sprinkle ¼ cup cinnamon mixture evenly over butter. Starting with 1 (9-inch) side, roll up dough jelly-roll fashion. Pinch ends and seam to seal. Place loaf, seam side down, in prepared pan, tucking ends under. Cover with towel; let rise in warm place about 1¼ hours or until doubled in bulk. (Dough should rise to top of pan.)

Preheat oven to 350°F. Combine reserved egg white and 1 tablespoon water in small bowl. Brush loaf with egg white mixture; sprinkle with reserved 1 tablespoon cinnamon mixture.

Bake 40 to 45 minutes or until loaf sounds hollow when tapped. Immediately remove from pan; cool completely on wire rack.

Makes 1 loaf

Cinnamon-Raisin Bread

Maple Nut Twist

1 recipe Sweet Yeast Dough (recipe follows)
2 tablespoons butter or margarine, melted
2 tablespoons honey
½ cup chopped pecans
¼ cup granulated sugar
2½ teaspoons maple extract, divided
½ teaspoon ground cinnamon
1 cup sifted powdered sugar
5 teaspoons milk

Prepare Sweet Yeast Dough; let rise as directed. Combine butter and honey in custard cup; set aside. Combine pecans, granulated sugar, 2 teaspoons maple extract and cinnamon in small bowl. Toss to coat; set aside.

Grease 2 baking sheets; set aside. Cut dough in half; cut half of dough into 2 pieces. Roll out 1 piece dough into 9-inch circle on lightly floured surface with lightly floured rolling pin. (Keep remaining dough covered with towel.) Place on prepared baking sheet. Brush half of butter mixture over dough. Sprinkle half of pecan mixture over butter.

Roll remaining piece dough into 9-inch circle. Carefully place dough over pecan filling, stretching dough as necessary to cover. Pinch edges to seal. Place 1-inch biscuit cutter* in center of circle as cutting guide, being careful not to cut through dough. Cut dough into 12 wedges with scissors or sharp knife, from edge of circle to edge of biscuit cutter, cutting through all layers. Pick up wide edge of 1 wedge, twist several times and lay back down on prepared sheet. Repeat twisting procedure with remaining 11 wedges. Repeat with remaining half of dough, butter mixture and pecan mixture. Cover coffee cakes with towel. Let rise in warm place about 1 hour or until doubled in bulk.

Preheat oven to 350°F. Bake on 2 racks in oven 20 to 25 minutes or until coffee cakes are golden brown and sound hollow when tapped. (Rotate baking sheets top to bottom halfway through baking.) Immediately remove from baking sheets; cool on wire racks about 30 minutes.

Combine powdered sugar, milk and remaining ½ teaspoon maple extract in small bowl until smooth. Drizzle over warm coffee cakes.
Makes 24 servings (2 coffee cakes)

*Or, use the lid of an herb jar if biscuit cutter is not available.

Sweet Yeast Dough

4 to 4¼ cups all-purpose flour, divided
½ cup sugar
2 packages active dry yeast
1 teaspoon salt
¾ cup milk
4 tablespoons butter or margarine
2 eggs
1 teaspoon vanilla

Combine 1 cup flour, sugar, yeast and salt in large bowl; set aside.

Combine milk and butter in 1-quart saucepan. Heat over low heat until mixture is 120° to 130°F. (Butter does not need to completely melt.) Gradually beat milk mixture into flour mixture with electric mixer at low speed. Increase speed to medium; beat 2 minutes. Reduce speed to low. Beat in eggs, vanilla and 1 cup flour. Increase speed to medium; beat 2 minutes. Stir in enough additional flour, about 2 cups, to make soft dough.

Turn out dough onto lightly floured surface; flatten slightly. Knead dough about 5 minutes or until smooth and elastic, adding ¼ cup more flour to prevent sticking if necessary. Shape dough into a ball; place in large greased bowl. Turn dough over so that top is greased. Cover with towel; let rise in warm place 1½ to 2 hours or until doubled in bulk. Punch down dough. Knead dough on lightly floured surface 1 minute. Cover with towel; let rest 10 minutes.

REFRIGERATOR SWEET YEAST DOUGH: Prepare Sweet Yeast Dough.

Shape dough into a ball; place in large greased bowl. Turn dough over so that top is greased. Cover with plastic wrap; refrigerate 3 to 24 hours. Punch down dough. Knead dough on lightly floured surface 1 to 2 minutes. Cover with towel; let dough rest 20 minutes before shaping and second rising. (Second rising may take up to 1½ hours.)

Maple Nut Twist

BAKING SECRET

Use large eggs for all recipes unless the ingredient list indicates another size.

Cinnamon Honey Buns

¼ cup butter or margarine, softened and divided
½ cup honey, divided
¼ cup chopped toasted nuts
2 teaspoons ground cinnamon
1 loaf (1 pound) frozen bread dough, thawed according to package directions
⅔ cup raisins

Grease 12 muffin cups with 1 tablespoon butter. To prepare honey-nut topping, mix together 1 tablespoon butter, ¼ cup honey and chopped nuts. Place 1 teaspoon topping in each muffin cup.

To prepare filling, mix together remaining 2 tablespoons butter, remaining ¼ cup honey and cinnamon. Roll out bread dough onto floured surface into 18×8-inch rectangle. Spread filling evenly over dough. Sprinkle evenly with raisins. Starting with long side, roll dough into log. Cut log into 12 (1½-inch) slices. Place 1 slice, cut-side up, into each prepared muffin cup. Set muffin pan in warm place; let dough rise 30 minutes.

Place muffin pan on foil-lined baking sheet. Bake at 375°F 20 minutes or until buns are golden brown. Remove from oven; cool in pan 5 minutes. Invert muffin pan to remove buns. *Makes 12 buns*

Favorite recipe from **National Honey Board**

Southwestern Biscuits

2¼ cups all-purpose flour
2 tablespoons granulated sugar
1 tablespoon baking powder
3 tablespoons butter or margarine, softened
1 cup (8-ounce can) cream-style corn
½ cup (4-ounce can) ORTEGA® Diced Green Chiles
1 egg, slightly beaten
1 tablespoon chopped fresh cilantro (optional)

COMBINE flour, sugar and baking powder in large bowl. Cut in butter with pastry blender or two knives until mixture resembles coarse crumbs.

STIR in corn, chiles, egg and cilantro; combine just until mixture holds together. Knead dough 10 times on well-floured surface. Pat dough into ¾-inch thickness. Cut into 3-inch biscuits. Place on greased baking sheets.

BAKE in preheated 400°F. oven for 20 to 25 minutes or until wooden pick inserted in center comes out clean. Let stand for 5 minutes; remove to wire racks to cool completely. *Makes 8 biscuits*

Tip: Serve these delicious biscuits with jalapeño butter. To make this spread with a kick, blend 1 to 2 teaspoons ORTEGA® Diced Jalapeños into ½ cup (1 stick) softened butter.

Cinnamon Honey Buns

Green Onion Cream Cheese Breakfast Biscuits

2 cups all-purpose flour
1 tablespoon baking powder
1 tablespoon sugar
¾ teaspoon salt
1 package (3 ounces) cream cheese
¼ cup vegetable shortening
½ cup finely chopped green onions
⅔ cup milk

1. Preheat oven to 450°F.

2. Combine flour, baking powder, sugar and salt in medium bowl. Cut in cream cheese and shortening with pastry blender or 2 knives until mixture resembles coarse crumbs. Stir in green onions.

3. Make well in center of flour mixture. Add milk; stir until mixture forms soft dough that clings together and forms a ball.

4. Turn out dough onto well-floured surface. Knead dough gently 10 to 12 times. Roll or pat dough to ½-inch thickness. Cut out dough with floured 3-inch biscuit cutter.

5. Place biscuits 2 inches apart on *ungreased* large baking sheet. Bake 10 to 12 minutes or until tops and bottoms are golden brown. Serve warm.

Makes 8 biscuits

Carrot Pecan Muffins

1¾ cups all-purpose flour
1 teaspoon baking soda
1 teaspoon ground cinnamon
¼ teaspoon ground nutmeg
1 cup sweetened applesauce
½ cup firmly packed light brown sugar
⅓ cup FLEISCHMANN'S® 70% Corn Oil Spread, melted
¼ cup EGG BEATERS® Healthy Egg Substitute
1 cup shredded carrots
½ cup pecan halves, chopped, divided
Powdered Sugar Glaze (recipe follows)

In small bowl, combine flour, baking soda, cinnamon and nutmeg; set aside.

In large bowl, combine applesauce, brown sugar, spread and Egg Beaters. Stir in flour mixture, carrots and ⅓ cup pecans just until moistened. Spoon batter into 12 lightly greased 2½-inch muffin-pan cups. Bake at 350°F for 20 to 25 minutes or until lightly browned. Cool on wire rack. Drizzle tops of muffins with Powdered Sugar Glaze; sprinkle with remaining pecans. *Makes 1 dozen muffins*

Prep time: 25 minutes
Cook time: 25 minutes

POWDERED SUGAR GLAZE: In small bowl, combine 1 cup powdered sugar and 5 to 6 teaspoons water until smooth.

Green Onion Cream Cheese Breakfast Biscuits

Lemon Poppy Seed Muffins

Lemon Poppy Seed Muffins

3 cups all-purpose flour
1 cup sugar
3 tablespoons poppy seeds
1 tablespoon grated lemon peel
2 teaspoons baking powder
1 teaspoon baking soda
½ teaspoon salt
1 container (16 ounces) plain low-fat yogurt
½ cup fresh lemon juice
¼ cup vegetable oil
2 eggs, beaten
1½ teaspoons vanilla

Preheat oven to 400°F. Grease 12 (3½-inch) large muffin cups; set aside.

Combine flour, sugar, poppy seeds, lemon peel, baking powder, baking soda and salt in large bowl. Combine yogurt, lemon juice, oil, eggs and vanilla in small bowl until well blended. Stir into flour mixture just until moistened. Spoon into prepared muffin cups, filling two-thirds full.

Bake 25 to 30 minutes or until wooden pick inserted in center comes out clean. Cool in pans on wire racks 5 minutes. Remove from pans. Cool on wire racks 10 minutes. Serve warm or cool completely.   *Makes 12 jumbo muffins*

Cheese & Herb Biscuits

- **4 cups all-purpose flour**
- **2 tablespoons sugar**
- **2 tablespoons baking powder**
- **1 teaspoon salt**
- **11 tablespoons butter or margarine, cold**
- **1¼ cups milk, cold**
- **Additional all-purpose flour**
- **1 cup (4 ounces) shredded Cheddar cheese**
- **½ cup chopped parsley or other fresh herbs**

Preheat oven to 425°F. Combine first 4 ingredients in large bowl. Cut butter into ¼-inch-thick chunks; add to flour mixture. Cut in butter with pastry blender or two knives until butter is broken into pea-size pieces. Make well in flour mixture; pour milk into well. Gently toss together with fork *just* until blended. *Do not overwork dough.*

Turn dough onto lightly floured work surface. To knead dough, gently pat or roll into ½-inch-thick rectangle; fold in half, adding more flour to work surface as needed to prevent sticking. Turn dough a ¼ turn. Repeat kneading at least 5 times, then sprinkle dough with cheese and herbs. Continue kneading dough until it is holds together and forms a soft dough.

Roll out dough to ½-inch thickness; cut out biscuits with 2-inch biscuit cutter. Place on lightly greased baking sheet, about ½ inch apart. Bake 15 to 20 minutes or until lightly browned. Cool slightly before removing from baking sheets. Serve warm.

Makes about 24 biscuits

Tip: Wrap leftover biscuits in foil and freeze. Reheat in foil in 325°F oven 10 minutes.

Serving suggestion: Brush tops with melted butter when removed from oven for an even more tender crust.

Favorite recipe from **Bob Evans Farms®**

Fiesta Corn Bread

- **2¼ cups all-purpose flour**
- **1¾ cups ALBERS® Yellow Corn Meal**
- **1½ cups (6 ounces) shredded Cheddar cheese**
- **1 cup (7-ounce can) ORTEGA® Diced Green Chiles**
- **½ cup granulated sugar**
- **2 tablespoons baking powder**
- **1½ teaspoons salt**
- **2 cups milk**
- **⅔ cup vegetable oil**
- **2 eggs, lightly beaten**

COMBINE flour, cornmeal, cheese, chiles, sugar, baking powder and salt in large bowl. Add milk, oil and eggs; stir just until moistened. Spread into greased 13×9-inch baking pan.

BAKE in preheated 375°F. oven for 30 to 35 minutes or until wooden pick inserted in center comes out clean. Cool in pan on wire rack for 10 minutes before serving.

Makes 20 servings

BAKING SECRET

Knead biscuit dough lightly (10 to 12 times) to bring it together for shaping. Too much kneading will make biscuits tough and mealy.

Coffee Walnut Chocolate Chip Muffins

½ cup (1 stick) butter or margarine, softened
½ cup granulated sugar
½ cup packed light brown sugar
2 to 3 tablespoons powdered instant coffee
2 teaspoons vanilla extract
1¾ cups all-purpose flour
1 tablespoon baking powder
½ teaspoon salt
2 eggs
⅔ cup milk
1½ cups coarsely chopped walnuts
¾ cup HERSHEY'S® Semi-Sweet Chocolate Chips

Heat oven to 350°F. Line twelve muffin cups (2½ inches in diameter) with paper bake cups. In large bowl, beat butter, granulated sugar, brown sugar, coffee and vanilla until creamy. Stir together flour, baking powder and salt. Beat together eggs and milk; add alternately with flour mixture to butter mixture, stirring just to combine. Stir in walnuts and chocolate chips. Fill muffin cups half full with batter. Bake 20 to 25 minutes. Cool 5 minutes; remove from pans to wire rack. Cool completely. *Makes 12 muffins*

Favorite Corn Muffins

1 cup all-purpose flour
¾ cup cornmeal
¼ cup bran
2 teaspoons baking powder
1½ teaspoons salt
½ teaspoon baking soda
1 cup dairy sour cream
2 eggs
¼ cup honey
¼ cup (½ stick) butter, melted

Preheat oven to 425°F. Coat 12-cup muffin pan generously with butter. Combine flour, cornmeal, bran, baking powder, salt and baking soda in large bowl. Beat sour cream, eggs, honey and butter in medium bowl until well blended. Add sour cream mixture to flour mixture; stir just until dry ingredients are evenly moistened. Spoon batter into prepared muffin cups. Bake 15 to 20 minutes. Cool in pan 5 minutes before removing. Serve warm.

Makes 12 muffins

Favorite recipe from **Wisconsin Milk Marketing Board**

Honey Zucchini Bread

1 egg
¾ cup honey
3 tablespoons vegetable oil
1 teaspoon vanilla
2½ cups all-purpose flour
1½ teaspoons baking powder
1 teaspoon grated orange peel
½ teaspoon baking soda
½ teaspoon ground ginger
¼ teaspoon salt
1½ cups grated zucchini
½ cup sunflower seeds

Beat egg slightly in large bowl. Add honey, oil and vanilla; mix well. Combine flour, baking powder, orange peel, baking soda, ginger and salt in medium bowl. Add flour mixture, zucchini and sunflower seeds to honey mixture; mix until well blended. Spoon batter into well greased 9×5×3-inch loaf pan. Bake at 325°F about 1 hour or until wooden pick inserted near center comes out clean. Cool 10 minutes in pan; remove from pan and cool completely.

Makes 12 servings

Favorite recipe from **National Honey Board**

Acknowledgments

Alpine Lace Brands, Inc.

Best Foods Division, CPC International Inc.

Blue Diamond Growers

Bob Evans Farms®

California Prune Board

California Tree Fruit Agreement

Cherry Marketing Institute, Inc.

Diamond Walnut Growers, Inc.

Dole Food Company, Inc.

Filippo Berio Olive Oil

Hershey Foods Corporation

Kraft Foods, Inc.

M & M/MARS

Nabisco, Inc.

National Honey Board

Nestlé USA

The Procter & Gamble Company

The Quaker® Kitchens

Southeast United Dairy Industry Association, Inc.

Sunkist Growers

Washington Apple Commission

Wisconsin Milk Marketing Board

Index

METRIC CONVERSION CHART

VOLUME MEASUREMENTS (dry)

$\frac{1}{8}$ teaspoon = 0.5 mL
$\frac{1}{4}$ teaspoon = 1 mL
$\frac{1}{2}$ teaspoon = 2 mL
$\frac{3}{4}$ teaspoon = 4 mL
1 teaspoon = 5 mL
1 tablespoon = 15 mL
2 tablespoons = 30 mL
$\frac{1}{4}$ cup = 60 mL
$\frac{1}{3}$ cup = 75 mL
$\frac{1}{2}$ cup = 125 mL
$\frac{2}{3}$ cup = 150 mL
$\frac{3}{4}$ cup = 175 mL
1 cup = 250 mL
2 cups = 1 pint = 500 mL
3 cups = 750 mL
4 cups = 1 quart = 1 L

VOLUME MEASUREMENTS (fluid)

1 fluid ounce (2 tablespoons) = 30 mL
4 fluid ounces ($\frac{1}{2}$ cup) = 125 mL
8 fluid ounces (1 cup) = 250 mL
12 fluid ounces (1$\frac{1}{2}$ cups) = 375 mL
16 fluid ounces (2 cups) = 500 mL

WEIGHTS (mass)

$\frac{1}{2}$ ounce = 15 g
1 ounce = 30 g
3 ounces = 90 g
4 ounces = 120 g
8 ounces = 225 g
10 ounces = 285 g
12 ounces = 360 g
16 ounces = 1 pound = 450 g

DIMENSIONS

$\frac{1}{16}$ inch = 2 mm
$\frac{1}{8}$ inch = 3 mm
$\frac{1}{4}$ inch = 6 mm
$\frac{1}{2}$ inch = 1.5 cm
$\frac{3}{4}$ inch = 2 cm
1 inch = 2.5 cm

OVEN TEMPERATURES

250°F = 120°C
275°F = 140°C
300°F = 150°C
325°F = 160°C
350°F = 180°C
375°F = 190°C
400°F = 200°C
425°F = 220°C
450°F = 230°C

BAKING PAN SIZES

Utensil	Size in Inches/Quarts	Metric Volume	Size in Centimeters
Baking or Cake Pan (square or rectangular)	8×8×2	2 L	20×20×5
	9×9×2	2.5 L	22×22×5
	12×8×2	3 L	30×20×5
	13×9×2	3.5 L	33×23×5
Loaf Pan	8×4×3	1.5 L	20×10×7
	9×5×3	2 L	23×13×7
Round Layer Cake Pan	8×1½	1.2 L	20×4
	9×1½	1.5 L	23×4
Pie Plate	8×1¼	750 mL	20×3
	9×1¼	1 L	23×3
Baking Dish or Casserole	1 quart	1 L	—
	1½ quart	1.5 L	—
	2 quart	2 L	—